The
Prospering
Soul

PART 1

BENJAMIN GIDEON

ISBN 979-8-88751-145-0 (paperback)
ISBN 979-8-88751-146-7 (digital)

Copyright © 2023 by Benjamin Gideon

All rights reserved. No part of this publication may be reproduced, distributed, or transmitted in any form or by any means, including photocopying, recording, or other electronic or mechanical methods without the prior written permission of the publisher. For permission requests, solicit the publisher via the address below.

Christian Faith Publishing
832 Park Avenue
Meadville, PA 16335
www.christianfaithpublishing.com

Printed in the United States of America

Beloved, I wish above all things that thou mayest prosper and be in health, even as thy soul prospereth.

—3 John 1:2 (KJV)

CONTENTS

Chapter 1: The Soul 1

Chapter 2: Vision 7

Chapter 3: Laughing All the Way 23

Chapter 4: Forgive Me, Forgive Me Not 33

Chapter 5: Permissible Versus Beneficial 42

Chapter 6: Convictions and Confessions 48

Chapter 7: Rest and Sleep 56

Chapter 8: Spiritual Anatomy 67

Chapter 9: Saying Yes Is Saying No 79

Chapter 10: Faith 87

Chapter 11: Change Your Angle 98

Chapter 12: We Need Jesus 104

CHAPTER 1

The Soul

So What Exactly Is It?

What is this metaphysical, miraculous substance that we have come to the knowledge of? This astounding, intrinsic, invaluable, and indispensable third part of every individual that breathes upon the face of the earth! This distinct part of the human identity that dwells somewhere among the body and the spirit; this supernatural phenomenon of our person, which evidences a realm beyond what the naked eye is capable of exploring. A place that encapsulates the mind, will and emotions, intellect, conscience, attitudes and the self; the internal mechanism which distinctly identifies an individual.

Let's start with an icebreaker: Wherever you are, at this very moment, please follow along and pick up your phone. Examine it for just a moment. Look at the casing, its color, shape, and the downloaded applications displayed on the screen. Now, in doing so, you've observed two-thirds of your phone. However, one-third of your phone has not been explored—the hardware. Without the hardware, you cannot host the software, and both the hardware and the software are housed within the casing.

Following the breadcrumbs of this thought, we've not only observed a phone, but also a prototype of the way we are comprised as people. The simple analogy of the smartphone, which reflects intelligence and purpose in its design, is accenting a deeper reality: human beings are created in a specific fashion. Since we are *Imago Dei* (the Latin term which means made in the image of God) we all have hardware (our spirit), software (our soul), and that which encases the two (our body). Each phone is intentionally branded with a logo to signify the originator of its design, and so it is with our beings. Since we are the design of God, made in His image, it is essential to pay attention to our soul, gaining understating regarding how it functions in correlation to the spirit and the body.

Bible Verses on Human Trichotomy

Below are examples of scriptures which attest to the enigma of the soul, apart from the body and spirit.

> For the word of God is quick, and powerful, and sharper than any two-edged sword, piercing even to the dividing asunder of soul and spirit, and of the joints and marrow, and is a discerner of the thoughts and intents of the heart. (Hebrews 4:12 KJV)

> And the very God of peace sanctify you wholly; and I pray God your whole spirit

and soul and body be preserved blameless unto the coming of our Lord Jesus Christ. (1 Thessalonians 5:23 KJV)

A Simple Encouragement for the Dichotomist

For those who hold a dichotomist perspective, this may be difficult to reconcile when speaking from the perspective of trichotomy. However, I implore you not to disallow what the Lord Jesus has allowed me to express in this book for the sake of edification and to bring His name glory. I do not disregard your convictions and beliefs on the matter of the soul and the spirit sharing one essence, yet still, I would ask that you proceed with confidence, knowing that if just one technique helps you to prosper your soul as you pursue the Lord, then it was worth your investment of time.

Where Did the Soul Come From?

> And the Lord God formed man of the dust of the ground, and breathed into his nostrils the breath of life; and man became a living soul. (Genesis 2:7 KJV)

It is expressly spoken that the soul comes from our Creator Himself—this invaluable substance, catalyzed by the precious breath of the living God, into His creation. The Hebrew word for soul is *nephesh* which means "that which breathes." It corresponds to the Greek word *psuchē*, which is usually translated "soul" or "life."

Even though the Word of God establishes that we have a soul, the question remains—why?

Why Have We Been Given a Soul?

We have been given a soul that we may be distinguishable among God's creation, to be uniquely included in expressing the image and nature of God (Father, Son, Holy Spirit). As God is three distinct persons sharing one divine essence and each person is God (not three forms of the same being, which is modalism), we have three distinct parts to our humanity. At our core, we are a spirit, we have a soul, and we are housed in a body. Therefore, we must discern a variety of factors in causing our entire person to flourish; many of these factors are rooted in the health of our soul.

Pay Attention to Your Soul

Since our soul is literally a third of our being, it is vital not to neglect our responsibilities in caring for it. We should always be alert and have an understanding on how to examine ourselves, having the ability to determine if our soul is healthy. Much of our ignorance is due to a culture which lacks the knowledge on curing issues of the soul. For this purpose, drugs are often prescribed to treat issues like depression, anxiety, and various issues that the human life combats. Now, this is not to diminish the importance of a prescription when there is true necessity. However, I'd like to suggest that much of the ways mankind aims to overcome spiritual issues, or issues of the soul, are incorrect. For this reason, many curable diseases of the soul cannot simply be overcome by physical means.

Opposition to the Soul

In the same sense that a digital virus or corrupted software can affect hardware and the programs designed to properly function within a computer, a virus compromising the health of our souls can affect our overall lives tremendously. These viruses often come through malware, a software that is designed to gain unauthorized access to a computer system, with ill intent. Viruses of the soul often invade our lives because we are ignorant in how to defend against them. Like a computer, our souls need proper security features that function similar to a computer's firewall. The Word of God declares to us: "Be sober, be vigilant; because your adversary the devil, as a roaring lion, walketh about, seeking whom he may devour" (1 Peter 5:8 KJV).

Upgraded Hardware = Upgraded Software

The realm of the spirit is where we deeply connect with God! When we receive the Lord, our spirit becomes one with the spirit of God. It can be likened to upgraded hardware, allowing for a greater capacity to download better software. Our responsibility is to download the greater software onto the hardware and to maximize the potential of our new system. Once we receive upgraded downloads, we must grow in knowledge of how something truly is intended to function.

> Now we have received not the spirit of the world, but the spirit which is of God; that we might know the things that are freely given to us of God. Which things also we speak, not in the words which man's wisdom teacheth, but which the

Holy Ghost teacheth; comparing spiritual things with spiritual. But the natural man receiveth not the things of the Spirit of God: for they are foolishness unto him: neither can he know them, because they are spiritually discerned. (1 Corinthians 2:12–14 KJV)

Without the Holy Spirit, His guidance, and His counsel, our souls are facing an alarming disadvantage.

Among the most sacred treasures that God grants us when we receive His spirit is purpose, along with knowledge and power to fulfill it, in relationship with Him. Purpose is the birthplace of vision.

CHAPTER 2

Vision

Where there is no vision, the people perish: but he that keepeth the law, happy is he. (Proverbs 29:18 KJV)

What a profound statement made by king Solomon in the Bible, and oh how true this statement is, especially the first half of this scripture! Vision is the specified road that is used by God to lead people to their destination, not allowing the person following this road to remain stagnant. Without it, one remains in a state of limbo and questions how to move forward in life.

Common Foundational Questions

Have you ever asked any of the following foundational questions: Who am I? What is my purpose? What do I do now? Where do I go? If you have, then guess what...you are a perfect candidate for the vision Jesus has for your life. Yes, God has the blueprints, plans, and the roadmap in His hands, and He wants to reveal them to you!

If you've ever purchased a new and tangible product, you may notice a few things that accompany the item purchased. You may find it appropriately packaged with some sort of box, wrapper, or etc. Now, good marketing will provide a logo somewhere on the item and one more thing, oh yeah, instructions on what do with and how to use the product purchased! Our lives are very similar to this product that you may now be visualizing.

We continually need proper instructions on how to operate and navigate through life. God knew that! That's why He gave us an instruction manual—the Holy Bible! This is to reveal and enable us to live our purpose—both general and specific—in relationship with God. You were created for a reason, and once that reason is discovered, vision is conceived!

What does purpose have to do with the health of our souls? The answer is simply everything! People who feel like they've lost their purpose, don't know their purpose, or have never walked in their purpose, often feel dead inside. When this season is elongated, it can lead to terrible side effects, ranging from lethargy, depression, apathy, and even suicide.

Purpose

Purpose is the *why* behind the *what*, while vision is the *how*.

Quick example: Someone wants to pursue a career in nursing (what). The general reason being that they are in need of finances. The specific reason is to compassionately comfort, heal, and alleviate the suffering of others. Both of these comprise the why. A nursing program, state examinations, internships or residencies, and applying for a suitable career at a desired medical facility are all pieces of vision (how).

God gives us a very simple answer for mankind's *general purpose:* "Let us hear the conclusion of the whole matter: Fear God, and keep his commandments: for this *is* **the whole** *duty* **of man**" (Ecclesiastes 12:13 KJV).

That's pretty simple to comprehend, but harder to apply.

So what is the simplest way to live this *general purpose?* Jesus reveals this to us in the gospels.

> Master, which is the great commandment in the law? Jesus said unto him, "Thou shalt love the Lord thy God with all thy heart, and with all thy soul, and with all thy mind. This is the first and great commandment. And the second is like unto it, Thou shalt love thy neighbour as thyself. On these two commandments hang all the law and the prophets." (Matthew 22:36–40 KJV)

Did you catch that? What an eye-opening conversation that we get a glimpse into! The entire purpose for mankind relates to these two commandments. This powerful outline is simple to grasp, yet only in relationship with Jesus and His people can we truly discover the intricacies regarding how to exude this lifestyle.

Therefore, vision is essential to life here on earth, and without it, we inwardly perish.

It's frustrating for someone to know what their *specific purpose* is, but to lack vision in fulfilling it. The discovery process, however, should not cause us grief, although it may often frustrate us into growth. Problems are intentionally presented because we are invited to seek God for solutions.

> It is the glory of God to conceal a thing:
> but the honour of kings is to search out a
> matter. (Proverbs 25:2 KJV)

We've been invited on one of the greatest treasure hunts in the history of our existence! Jesus is the treasure, but as we seek Him and find Him, He begins to add the building blocks on how we can express Him in our day-to-day lives through our designated purpose. Our souls have been intricately designed to seek out these answers until they are revealed. For this reason, many are spiritually hindered in their future when purpose and vision are absent. After all, it is a rarity to find things that we are not intentionally searching for.

Once vision is obtained, it is important to differentiate it from a goal. A goal can be compared to milestones on the way to your destination, vision is the specific road you're taking to the destination, and purpose is the *why* fueling your endeavor to the specific destination. Why a chef, a pastor, a teacher? Why stay in the marriage, adopt the baby, or leave the job? Vision presents choices, as we make effective decisions on the road to effectuate purpose.

Wandering Versus Seeking

If it's not obvious yet, God did not create His people to be wanderers; He created us to be seekers! Seeking is an imperative prerequisite to vision. So then, what is the difference between a seeker and a wanderer? Wandering simply has no aim, whereas seeking intends to hit an intended target or at least to get within range. Wandering is more spontaneous than it is directional.

For example, I can wander around the mall with no intention of purchasing anything, but upon stumbling across something that I enjoy, like, or admire, I may decide to acquire the item. Seeking is about intention! I am going to the mall for the purpose of upgrading my wardrobe. I want new jeans (within range of the target). I desire a new pair of black, fitted jeans which are a size 32 men's waistline and 31 inches in length (the bull's-eye of the target).

Wandering delays solution and becomes an obstacle to growth; whereas, properly seeking draws breakthroughs closer. This statement, however, should not be understood to cancel spontaneity every once in a while. Life cannot be unalterable due to our plans for each moment, down to the finest detail. We don't want to be robbed of the joy that God distributes in surprises.

How God Distributes Vision

When I was in high school, I was heavily influenced by hip-hop culture. I enjoyed the break dancing (b-boy), the graffiti (I only tagged a few times), the emceeing (getting on the mic to rap) or hosting a concert, and the DJ. These are the four pillars of hip-hop. As I was being slowly transformed by the Holy Spirit, my focus began to shift from the culture of hip-hop to its spiritual condition. I began to notice the derogatory lyrics, the murderous messages, the drug-induced subculture, and God began to burden my heart! When a burden remains, it's usually because God is calling us to partner with Him, in order to bring a specific solution to a specific problem. I began to cry out for two years that God would use me to change the music that the world was listening to—that's purpose. Yet I was lacking vision.

So in those two years, I wrote music privately in my room to hip-hop instrumentals. I practiced a variety of verbal techniques and studied many successful artists that inspired me. After two years, through a long series of events, God granted me the opportunity to enter into a studio and record my first album at age seventeen and eighteen. Following this, the Lord granted me the platform I eagerly requested.

I began to perform at local events, record albums, shoot music videos, get interviewed by various media sources and network throughout the Christian circles in the industry. God opened doors to work with reputable organizations and affiliated me with numerous churches, as the gospel was joyfully spread instead of demonic rhetoric spewed on the radio.

It's been over a decade now that I get to make the smallest of impacts regarding hip-hop as a Christian artist that ministers Jesus into hip-hop culture.

One Step at a Time

You see, vision from God always accompanies the purpose He's placed in your heart. That purpose is always for His glorification and for someone's edification. We never see the complete picture; we only see glimpses. Therefore, God distributes vision step by step. If we don't take one step, we will not receive the next.

> For we know in part, and we prophesy in part. (1 Corinthians 13:9 KJV)

I remember walking to a view that I enjoy by my house. It was earlier in the morning, and the road was surrounded by thick fog. I was unable to adequately make out anything beyond approximately thirty feet in front of me. As I continued walking, God was making me aware that this is the same way He grants vision. As we keep walking, He keeps supplying the steps regarding our purpose.

Community

Another way to receive vision from God frequently includes community. I remember serving at a church where we had a worship leader that I was friends with. She and my sister planned to hang out, and I was unaware that she was coming over. I was worshiping God via singing in my room and had also been crying out for the Lord to give me a decent voice to worship Him with for a few years. I became determined to sing to God daily as an act of faith, until my request was fulfilled. When she was walking toward my sister's room (mine is next to hers) she asked my sister, "Who is that singing? He has a soulful voice." When she knew it was me, she was surprised and said, "You can sing?"

Now this may not seem significant on the surface, but my prayer was answered, yet I could not verify it on my own. I lacked confidence to sing before others, and I wasn't going to do so anytime soon. God used my friend to call out what was hidden to the eyes of my heart. When I was enlightened to the realization that this prayer was fulfilled, it opened the doors of vision for where this voice could be used. For this purpose, my third album titled *Please Help* (my stage name is R3fugee, pronounced "refugee") contains much more singing than my first two and aided me in delivering the gospel in newer realities artistically.

Who you're accountable to will often aid in casting vision for you. This should be tested and followed when it aligns with the Word of God. If they are trustworthy and their life bears the fruit that you intend to also obtain, keep your ears open for vision that God may grant through their advice. Countless times, the application of these scriptures has gained me much:

> Wherefore, my beloved brethren, let every man be swift to hear, slow to speak, slow to wrath. (James 1:19 KJV)

> The way of a fool is right in his own eyes: but he that hearkeneth unto counsel is wise. (Proverbs 12:15 KJV)

Even Jesus casted vision for all of us in *the Great Commission,* found in Matthew 28:16–20 and Mark 16:15–

18. He even prayed and cast vision for every future believer in John 17. For these reasons, who you align with matters. They can progress you or deter you in fulfilling your purpose. Sometimes it's necessary to un-align from some, simply to realign with the right people. If you should take this route, do it with prayer and caution.

Stages of Vision

Vision is made up of three basic stages. God revealed this to me at a conference in San Diego, California, in 2020. During the conference, I was crying out that God would give me *new vision*. However, His response was surprising. God did not want to give me new vision; He wanted me to *receive renewed vision*. He had already spoken concerning what He desired me to do. The revelation took even deeper root as the Lord allowed me to observe others receiving new vision and renewed vision. Then is where it was made evident that many of us have suffered from a *loss of vision*.

New vision is simply a heavenly download that is revealed to us for the first time. Our heart often passionately burns to see the things of the spirit become tangible as soon as it is made known. It is followed by a demand for growth in God and a greater dependency upon Him to help us make it a reality. Your mind is often captivated by it, and your soul emits the emotions of nervousness, excitement, and expectation. New vision must be diligently guarded and not immediately published publicly. Pray before revealing new information because Satan loves destroying things in their infancy before they reach their fullness, since at infancy, they are not a threat.

> Give not that which is holy unto the dogs, neither cast ye your pearls before swine, lest they trample them under their feet, and turn again and rend you. (Matthew 7:6 KJV)

Loss of vision, therefore, occurs when we have vision trampled on, when we become stagnant in advancing, and when we give up because of numerous obstacles. Prematuring that which is not yet ripe is another factor which contributes to loss. In fact, there are a variety of reasons that may lead to vision loss, including disconnecting from Jesus, community, and His Word. Furthermore, the wrong environment can hinder what God desires us to birth. Most people don't birth their children in a fast-food restaurant simply because it is an unsustainable environment to receive new life. The hospital bed is an appropriate environment for new birth. Your environment contributes greatly to the fruition of the vision.

A Personal Example of a Loss of Vision

I recall when God was birthing a deep cry in me to see homeless people fed, clothed, and prayed for. I was at a local restaurant in town with my girlfriend at the time, and I was ecstatic to share what was brewing in my heart over dinner! After all, she was my "best friend."

However, between platters of appetizers and a delicious meal, I would also be served with a broken heart. As I excitedly shared new vision with her, I was hoping she would enthusiastically receive the news, maybe even refine the vision and help me with the details. Yet when she finished hearing me out, her response was more of an irritation and critical questioning of logistics. Up to that point, I only knew the purpose and deeply desired to conceive the vision with her.

The vision was trampled on and miscarried into existence. Had I known it would take years to renew what was lost that night, I would have remained silent, even before my "best friend." I learned the hard way that we must guard the things of heaven actively and take them seriously. Miscarrying vision is costly to your soul. It feels like something dies on the inside. If you find yourself in the loss of vision stage, don't grieve too long.

This brings us to renewed vision which, in my estimation, is the most profound. God often restores that which was lost and inspires us by adding a simple detail that inspires us to keep going. Our Father knows what we need! He's so good! In Jesus, what was lost can be found again! The Holy Ghost can breathe into the dead things and cause them to come alive! He will provide the strength, the inspiration, and the people. Don't lose heart! If you're praying for something God no longer wishes to renew, then ask Him for something new that He wishes to fulfill. When was the last time you asked God to renew vision?

There's one more thing regarding the three stages of vision, one underlying factor that blankets all three: the responsibility of maintaining a vision.

Maintaining a vision looks different for each person. However, the concept is simple: to continue doing your part in pushing forward even when things seem stagnant or arduous. Most people don't quit their job because it currently inconveniences them, especially if they need it! They continue pushing through hardship and pain because their need is greater than the difficulty. In the same way, we don't quit our families every time we are not in the best of circumstances. We aim to work things out!

So when things get tough, don't abandon your vision, maintain it! Remember, it's the roadmap to fulfilling your purpose! Sometimes all God asks us to do is to keep doing what He's already commissioned us to do. When you are working to maintain the vision He gave you, He is working to maintain you!

Renewed, Refreshed, Restored

Frequently, even while we have purpose and vision, we need them to be refreshed because they are not short in nature. Back to the analogy of the car on the road—long journeys require stops for food and gas. It's not an *if* but a *when* regarding stopping, refueling, and refreshing.

The Lord encouraged and instructed us through the apostle Paul stating: "And let us not be weary in well doing: for in due season we shall reap, if we faint not" (Galatians 6:9 KJV).

Furthermore, He taught us how not to grow weary, through the prophet Isaiah: "But they that wait upon the Lord shall renew their strength; they shall mount up with wings as eagles; they shall run, and not be weary; and they shall walk, and not faint" (Isaiah 40:31 KJV).

Waiting on the Lord is key to renewing vision, not to mention, receiving it. If we are impatient, we run the high risk of miscarrying what heaven desires to impregnate us with. If we have unhealthy souls, we cannot bring fourth the vision which surrounds our purpose. We must be renewed, refreshed, and restored constantly.

Simple Ways to Manifest Vision

As established, vision is extremely healthy for the soul, as it provides a roadmap for purpose. Here are a few simple steps that can help us to manifest the mandates of heaven, partnering with God to birth them. After spending serious time *seeking* Him in prayer, write it down.

> And the LORD answered me, and said, Write the vision, and make it plain upon tables, that he may run that readeth it. (Habakkuk 2:2 KJV)

The prophet Habakkuk is instructed not only to write down the vision from God, but to write it plainly, in a way that he who reads it may understand and relay it. Therefore, when you write down what you believe God is laying up in your heart, document it in such a way that it does not lose its inspiration and clarity. That way, once it is presented to an audience, they can grab a hold of it and help propel it into existence. Writing down the vision is the first step to taking something on the inside of you and bringing it outside of you.

Secondly, writing it down serves as a record to the vision, which holds the one receiving it accountable to working it out with God. This is where action steps are required.

Act on It

> For as the body without the spirit is dead, so faith without works is dead also. (James 2:26 KJV)

Prayer and writing down the vision must be the foundational steps for our actions, but they are not the actions themselves. When God allowed me to rap for His glory, I had to connect with people, record in the studio, write the lyrics, and *do* a host of other tasks regarding the vision I obtained from Him. God did not do this for me. He provided me with the materials I needed to build His vision, and the spirit of God opened the doors of supernatural favor that I did not have the keys to naturally open.

He built the vision on the inside, but I was responsible to manifest it outwardly. In this way, the world could see what was unseen and give God glory. I could not *leap* into this assignment from God; I had to *take steps* into it. Not every vision can be executed like a cannonball jump into a pool; some vision has to be tiptoed into. The main objective is to take the step and pray for strategy as you do so.

Teamwork Makes the Dream Work

Let's say it's the day of Thanksgiving and you have been tirelessly working on dinner since the morning. You are expecting to host many guests, and therefore, you prepare a ton of food! If you're like me, you're thinking of sweet potatoes, turkeyzilla (my made-up name for a giant turkey) and cranberry sauce, with a really enticing gravy. Don't forget the King Hawaiian semi-toasted buns and the variety of foods that adorn the table. Is your mouth watering? I'm not gonna lie, mine is! Now that we are hungry, let's fill up with some truth since it may not be Thanksgiving just yet!

To continue this hypothetical scenario, you sit at the table and everyone sits down with you. You pray and thank God for the provision, then start digging into your plate. Now imagine for a moment, that after a few bites, you boldly stand upon the table and announce that everyone should cease eating. How weird would that be!

Let's alter the scenario for a moment. Version 2: After a few mouthfuls, you notice that those surrounding you have halted from eating and are simply watching you eat…awkward! You ask, "Why isn't anyone eating?" They simply reply, "Only those who cooked the meal should eat it." We are all aware (I hope) that this scenario is hypothetical and is not bound to happen.

However, if we frame this same concept spiritually, this tends to happen all too frequently. We hoard the vision of God to ourselves, only to watch it die in arms that could not accommodate its magnitude. It either grows too large or remains too small to sustain.

You see, vision from God always involves others. We are not called to birth it alone. It is not cliché then to admit that teamwork truly does make the dream work. Yet be prayerful about who you select to help you with vision. Do not be hasty or desperate. God will provide for the work He's called you to do. When it's His will, it's His bill. When it's of His spirit, He will do the heavy lifting. No one person can perform the fullness of the works of God, except God Himself.

The Wrap-Up on Vision

In conclusion, healthy vision is a factor of a healthy soul. Do not aim so high that you are disappointed due to delusion, and do not aim so low that you can do things in your own power. Let your vision be built on a string of long-term and short-term goals that feed the purpose behind it. If you fail, get up and try again.

> Trust in the Lord with all thine heart; and lean not unto thine own understanding. In all thy ways acknowledge him, and he shall direct thy paths. (Proverbs 3:5–6 KJV)

CHAPTER 3

Laughing All the Way

You know those deep, gut-wrenching laughs that make your stomach hurt, your face muscles stretch, and your smile expand from ear to ear? Those laughs that make you gasp for air because something was heard through your ears, tickled your soul, and produced a joyful noise that was amplified through your mouth? You know…the kind where you see those baby videos of the kid laughing hysterically and then letting out shouts of enthusiastic laughter, only to be reciprocated by you shortly after. Wow… I sounded kind of like Dr. Seuss with that last sentence. Moving on now! How about the kind of wind-up laughs where it starts with a simple chuckle, then another chuckle, then chuck, chuck, chuckle, and then becomes an eruption of enjoyability voiced through sound? It starts like a locomotive and then gets rolling.

If you happen to be smiling at this time, take a moment to thank God. Seriously, just pause for a second and thank God. For the super-spiritual please *Selah* (lighthearted joke). Think of what a wonderful God we serve. Would a God who designed laughter and smiling, deep joy and gut-wrenching, hysterical laughter ever delight in people suffering? Laughter and smiling are miniature testimonies that God deeply desires His people to live in joy! I imagine that God often laughs and smiles along with His children! Some of our laughs—the kind that may be piercing and obnoxious to some ears; yes, these ones—are so precious to the heart of God.

In fact, I believe these laughs were tuned at the perfect pitch and frequency when God created us, simply to bring the Lord pleasure. In the same way we watch videos of people laughing and laugh ourselves, I'm persuaded that the Lord is similar, in that He also laughs at and with us, as He is watching us operate in the day.

Now when I say God is laughing at you, I'm not saying that He laughs at your pain, struggles, and things you take seriously. What I am saying is that when something is pure, lovely, lighthearted, and not a perversion of truth, when you mean to say a word and pronounce it funny, I believe the Lord takes pleasure in these simple moments with us. In fact, so does scripture: "Thou art worthy, O Lord, to receive glory and honour and power: for thou hast created all things, and for thy pleasure they are and were created" (Revelation 4:11 KJV).

So what does scripture say specifically about laughter? What am I even basing my reasoning on? When should we laugh? Does God want us to laugh? Does God Himself actually laugh?

> A time to weep, and a time to laugh;
> a time to mourn, and a time to dance.
> (Ecclesiastes 3:4 KJV)

Our amazing God has given us a time to laugh! If you are not familiar with Ecclesiastes 3, it is a famous chapter in the Word of God that many are familiar with, but not many of us know how to apply effectively. This passage is very clear that God has framed things within time, and believe me, God has greatly graced man in doing this.

When to Laugh and What to Laugh About

So when should we laugh? Most of the time, we can take a common-sense approach, but sometimes we need to be alerted to specific situations. For example, laughing at a funeral for any unwarranted reason is highly inappropriate. Yet if during the funeral, a funny story was told to shed light on the deceased's life, this would provide an invitation for laughter. Moreover, if it's a celebration of life service, we are invited to rejoice, even as we are sensitive to the mourning of others.

Another example includes when your dad, teacher, pastor, or other fatherly figure aims to tell you a "dad joke" and it's not funny…cue the crickets. Even though you may not laugh, that time is allotted for you to do so. These tiny examples of the time regarding laughter are often ingrained within us due to cultural norms. As obvious as these scenarios may seem, some scenarios are dubious to us.

> Nor should there be obscenity, foolish talk or coarse joking, which are out of place, but rather thanksgiving. (Ephesians 5:4 NIV)

Let me make something clear and eliminate confusion: God is not okay with perverted jokes, jokes that involve cursing, racist jokes, jokes that demean a person, jokes about people going to hell, or jokes that downplay a person's actual pain. All of this kind of joking does not belong in the kingdom of God.

That means some of your favorite comedians may not be the most beneficial to your soul! If you find yourself repeating perverted jokes, cussing as they do to get an audience to laugh, you're actually opposing your soul. So should you never watch a comedy show again, since the industry is saturated with perversion and cursing?

Well, have you ever researched Christian comedy? There are actually a variety of acts that are in accordance with kind of jokes God wants us to pay attention to, and they are *not* corny! What you sow within you, you will reap later, so choose life for your soul.

> Death and life are in the power of the tongue: and they that love it shall eat the fruit thereof. (Proverbs 18:21 KJV)

What are you letting speak over you, hiding behind the context of a joke?

> Do not be deceived: God cannot be mocked. A man reaps what he sows. For he that soweth to his flesh shall of the flesh reap corruption; but he that soweth to the Spirit shall of the Spirit reap life everlasting. (Galatians 6:7–8 KJV)

In no way am I aiming to take away your joy, but in all ways I am suggesting that you take inventory of the things you laugh at. Laugher is a clear indicator that your soul is responding. That's why even our laughter should be welcoming for the Holy Ghost to be a part of. When God is around, there is more joy, not less.

> For the kingdom of God is not eating and drinking, but righteousness and peace and joy in the Holy Spirit, (Romans 14:17 KJV)

Surrendering what we laugh at may be difficult at first, but this will cause us to reflect the Lord brighter and better to those around us. Think of your children and the jokes you say around them, maybe even to them. Do those jokes build them up? Do your jokes tear them down? What are you allowing to dwell in your soul because it entered in by a trojan horse joke?

What God Laughs At

> The wicked plot against the righteous and gnash their teeth at them; but the Lord laughs at the wicked, for he knows their day is coming. (Psalm 37:12–13 KJV)

Wait… God laughs at the wicked? Apparently…yes! As a cruel person laughs at and persecutes God's people…Christ is being persecuted with us, and God will not be mocked.

Although the above paragraph states that God laughs at the wicked, it is imperative to be aware that it's not God's will that the wicked suffer or are destroyed (2 Peter 3:9), but that He laughs at their plans because His plan will prevail if the righteous obey.

> For they intended evil against thee: they imagined a mischievous device, which they are not able to perform. (Psalm 21:1 KJV)

Here we see how these two schools of thought intertwine because those who aim to mock God, or His people, end up mocking themselves. Therefore, it is important that you guard your soul from what you laugh at because we will be held accountable to God as well. Moreover, be careful who you laugh at and the reason behind your laughter. God is watching.

Plan to Laugh

Throughout His word, God has made clear, that His desire is for us to rejoice, celebrate, delight, shout for joy, and enjoy Him.

> Rejoice in the Lord always: and again I say, Rejoice! (Philippians 4:4 KJV)

Every generation receives this privilege in the Lord if they choose Him. For God to command us to do these things will require the gift of laughter, although we may not feel like we are able to laugh, rejoice, celebrate, delight, etc. at times. Have you noticed that the narrative of Satan is to start the day off in negativity? To cause us to hold onto the negative of the day instead of measuring the day the Lord has made properly?

We cannot surrender our joy! Therefore, let laughter and joy be on the menu of your day. David and Solomon both understood that joy is a choice, not a feeling. King David planned that he would rejoice and be glad in his day. Do we do that?

> This is the day which the Lord hath made; we will rejoice and be glad in it. (Psalm 118:24 KJV)

> A merry heart does good, like medicine, But a broken spirit dries the bones. (Proverbs 17:22 NKJV)

If you've not planned to laugh, I challenge you to begin your day with this in mind: to thank God that you woke up and that He gave you a new day, to rejoice and delight in the fact that no matter how you feel, you are in relationship with God. If we surrender the joy of the Lord, we surrender the strength that comes through it. Joy, rejoicing, and laughter are some of the distributors of God's strength in our lives.

> …For the joy of the Lord is your strength. (Nehemiah 8:10 KJV)

Laughter Is Attractive

It's almost always the people who have the smile on their face, those who crack lighthearted jokes, and are able to hope for the best, regardless of their circumstances that attract us. We want to be their friends because we want in on that joy! Have you noticed that they are usually the ones comfortable enough to make the first move toward relationship? They seem, if anything, to exhibit freedom. Their soul is not weighed down with the cares of life, even after discovering that they too have issues behind their welcoming smile.

If we were to think about it from an employment standpoint, most employers wish to hire the upbeat, energetic visionary that makes people feel welcome. The entitled and frowning candidates are rarely the ones placed before customers. Your facial expressions speak a language of their own. What has yours been saying lately? Who wants a Jesus that never laughs, smiles, or jokes? If we are His representatives on earth, it's time we start growing into the freedom of Jesus. Laugh a little more; it's actually good for you and nourishes your soul!

The truth is, many are depressed, in terrible circumstances, pained, hurting, or disgruntled, aiming to escape their reality. So how does someone in these conditions laugh? If anything, laughter is an indicator of hope. Even those around us who smile, laugh, and display freedom often deal with numerous issues that we will never retain knowledge of. However, their approach to suffering may be different than ours.

Personally speaking, sometimes things are so overwhelming, all I can do is pray, cry, and eventually laugh. I laugh sometimes not because I'm happy, but simply because I've cried all the tears I have! At that point, I'm reminded that Jesus and I are together in the storm, and regardless of my circumstances, I choose—to the best of my ability—to hope against hope. When I laugh in my pain, I can't help but believe that hell shudders because God Himself is laughing in us and through us. I know it may sound crazy and I promise that it does not happen often, but when it does, I know God is already working out the solution.

A Few Facts on Laughter

1) Laughter allows for endorphins in our brains to stimulate euphoria, similar to a narcotic, minus the negative side effects.
2) Socially laughing is like a wildfire. If you're in an environment for laughter, like when someone yawns, you will be influenced to laugh as well. We were created to laugh with others.
3) Laughter is foundational to romantic relationships. Remember how we discussed laughter as being attractive? Well, women find men more attractive if they can make them laugh. Men, in turn, find it easier to be around women who laugh with them.
4) Have you heard of serotonin? It's considered to be a chemical that is found in antidepressants. When we laugh, little bits of this chemical is released to help regulate our mood. Laughing, therefore, can aid in healthy brain function.
5) It's not just your head! Obviously, when you're laughing, you're not as stressed as you'd normally be. Laughing produces effects that help reduce inflammation in blood vessels and heart muscles. This can prevent various health issues of the heart.

6) As with most exercises, a good amount of laughing can help combat your calorie rate. It may take a lot of it, but it sure helps!
7) Those jokes that leave people gasping for air actually oxygenate the body. Keep laughing!

Laughing is an essential part of the human experience, because God and people both laugh. We connect with divine design when making this joyful noise, especially in God's presence. It is a form of freedom that was given to us to further enhance our walks with God and others, enjoying them even more than we already do. I can't imagine Jesus being extremely serious all the time, but instead, being the guest of honor and the life of most of the parties He attended. Are we walking in His joy and laughter?

If not, we have the opportunity to reset our days, choosing to rejoice, to be glad, and to laugh. In fact, ask the Lord Jesus to reveal to you His joy in this day! What do you have to lose? On the contrary, you have so much to gain, even for your overall health! Even though we may not be "dashing through the snow" on a sleigh pulled by horses, through powdery, white blanketed fields, we should still aim to be "laughing all the way."

CHAPTER 4

Forgive Me, Forgive Me Not

Let me tell you a true story. These lessons are some of the treasures that God has revealed to me in my walk with Him, and I'd like to share them with you. It must have been my first or second year in college at California State University of Northridge. Shout out to all the matadors! At this time in my life I was dating someone that was very special to me. She and I were in the first year of dating, and I was in prayer, which is my normal morning routine.

During prayer time, the Lord began to speak to me and said (paraphrasing the best I remember), "Whenever someone entrusts you with their heart, it becomes yours. If you break it, you are responsible for fixing it. There are two hearts that you've broken, and you need to ask for forgiveness." I was so shocked that the Lord cared about relationships that ran their course and were no longer in operation. I could not fathom the purpose of what the Lord was asking me to do; however, I would learn much about forgiveness in the coming interactions between these two women and Jesus.

Key point: Jesus did not start this lesson at the offense others caused me. He started by confronting my heart and holding me accountable for the pain that I caused them.

It Starts With Us

> And why do you look at the speck in your brother's eye, but do not consider the plank in your own eye? Or how can you say to your brother, 'Let me remove the speck from your eye'; and look, a plank is in your own eye? Hypocrite! First remove the plank from your own eye, and then you will see clearly to remove the speck from your brother's eye. (Matthew 7:3–5 NKJV)

We should always deal with the offense toward others in us before we even think of confronting the offense others have caused us. A healthy soul absolutely cannot be rooted in offense. It will rot the fruit of the Holy Ghost in you and others. Let's deal with us first…others second. We must not forget what the Word of God says: "Follow peace with all men, and holiness, without which no man shall see the Lord: Looking diligently lest any man fail of the grace of God; lest any root of bitterness springing up trouble you, and thereby many be defiled" (Hebrews 12:14–15 KJV).

It's crazy to think that our actions can affect others so deeply, that we can cause others to be defiled by our own bitterness. To summarize what the Word of God is saying in a nutshell: Bitterness is a contagious spiritual disease that we must be healed from in order to prevent harming others, who can become carriers of our sickness. Therefore, we must be careful in the way we speak, act, and behave—always checking our own hearts with the Great Physician. Now you're probably wondering about or criticizing the story that has no middle or end at the opening of this chapter, so let's continue.

The two hearts I broke were revealed to me by name. Immediately afterward, I was instructed to reach out to those two girls and write them a letter of apology, bathed in complete honesty and humility. So I did what any brave and sincere general of the kingdom would do… Facebook Messenger, duh! As a young man this was the tool at my disposal, and it was good enough to take the words of God's heart into theirs, as God would begin to mend wounds that I caused.

Key point: God's Word is always followed by an action. We must work out what the Holy Ghost works in.

Now let's code name one of the girls *J* and the second one *T*. The letter I wrote to J went forth first. I admitted to her the honest reason why I left our relationship in tenth grade. I confessed that as a young man I was interested in dating other people and that I felt unwelcomed by some people in her family. The root of my mistreatment and lack of sincerity in leaving the relationship was rooted in immaturity, both as a man and a man of God. After a long letter expressing these things and asking for forgiveness, I eagerly awaited J's response.

To my surprise and to the glory of God, J responded in a manner that I have not since forgotten. She upheld and esteemed my character. Kindness, deeply rooted in appreciation surrounded the words in her reply. She expressed how she had been waiting to hear the truth in these words since tenth grade. How these words brought her the closure that she was looking for. Not only was there forgiveness, but now peace and the opportunity for reconciliation.

God wowed me that day! I could not believe that I was the reason for someone's grief for three to four years. The only thing it took to begin the healing process was genuine repentance of my harmful actions, a humble request for forgiveness, along with honesty to have an open conversation. I was so shocked and perceived the value of this woman I had once betrayed. She graced me when she had every right to grill me.

Love Is the Antidote for Self-Righteousness

Over the years, the Lord has made it increasingly clear to me that He is more concerned with His children being righteous than being right. It delights Him more when we become love and reveal grace in places where we believe we have the right to remain offended.

> Therefore if you bring your gift to the altar, and there remember that your brother has something against you, leave your gift there before the altar, and go your way. First be reconciled to your brother, and then come and offer your gift. (Matthew 5:23–24 NKJV)

> Dearly beloved, avenge not yourselves, but rather give place unto wrath: for it is

written, Vengeance is mine; I will repay, saith the Lord. (Romans 12:19 KJV)

We always have a choice. We can get the revenge on our own and produce wickedness in the process, or we can let our Heavenly Father get revenge in His way and timing. You never know…your worst enemy can even become your greatest ally. God has sent multiple people to apologize to me years after they've caused offense, even though it was forgiven long ago. He sent them simply to make me aware that He did not forget my pain. In turn, we must never forget this truth: "For if ye forgive men their trespasses, your heavenly Father will also forgive you: But if ye forgive not men their trespasses, neither will your Father forgive your trespasses" (Matthew 6:14–15 KJV).

This brings me to T. T and I dated for the first half of my senior year of high school, and the wound may have been a little more fresh than when I was instructed to apologize to J. At this point in time, T was in a relationship with another person. Let's call him K. Out of respect for T, God granted me the wisdom to directly message K so that there would be nothing hidden behind his back. I entrusted him with the message to give to her and waited anxiously, eager to know her reply, hoping to be cleared of my mistakes.

After a short time, I received an extremely long message from her. T cussed me out, called me a few different names, etc. Guess what…she had every right! I deserved the things spoken about me, whether they were due to immaturity, disrespectful behavior, etc. Although I did not deserve everything spoken in her response, I did not hold her accountable for her harsh response. I broke her heart…not the other way around. To make matters worse, my friend's girlfriend and T were good friends. Well, my friend decided he wanted to break up with his girlfriend at the same time! Even though I advised against it, we broke up with them on the same day, maybe one or two hours apart. I highly recommend that no one do that. It's messed up!

I found myself at a fork in the road. Was I forgiven or not? I needed to know, and the suspense was causing me anxiety. I turned to the Lord in desperation and asked Him something like, "Lord, do you forgive me? She clearly did not." He replied similarly to this statement: "Yes, you've done your part, so I forgive you. Now it's on her to forgive." What a relief! I'm telling you…there is nothing more comforting than affirmation from God after you've obeyed Him. What an unforgettable experience!

Forgiveness Versus Reconciliation

Sometimes all we can do is surrender the situation back to God. We cannot force anyone to forgive us. However, there's a distinction between forgiveness and reconciliation that I recently learned. Forgiveness does not require two people, but simply one. It does not demand entering into relationship with the offender again, but reconciliation does. You cannot have relationship with an offender without reconciling. The two parties must come to a mutual forgiveness and agreement. The Lord also does not command us to be reconciled unto everyone, but gives us this command instead: "Repay no one evil for evil. Have regard for good things in the sight of all men. If it is possible, as much as depends on you, live peaceably with all men" (Romans 12:17–18 NKJV).

Sometimes peace comes solely through forgiveness, but reconciliation is the greater of the two. If you cannot attain either or, aim to obtain peace, for we are left with a blessing when peace is grasped by both the offender and the offended.

> Blessed are the peacemakers: for they shall be called the children of God. (Matthew 5:9 KJV)

Although peace rarely appears without a fight or a struggle, it is necessary for the benefit of our soul. Peace is one of the fruits of the Holy Ghost, and without it, our soul has no order. The peace of God surpasses all understanding, and often, we cannot enter into this gracious gift when holding someone under the waters of unforgiveness. The paradox is that the harder and longer we hold them under that water, the more we suffocate internally.

Forgiveness Requires Maturity

Once we understand how much we've truly been forgiven, it actually becomes hard not to forgive. The Holy Ghost drives out anything that does not look like Jesus. That's why Satan aims to create a stronghold inside of us; he doesn't want to leave!

However, we are actually called to demolish strongholds, just like Jesus. Look at what He says: "For this purpose the Son of God was manifested, that he might destroy the works of the devil" (1 John 3:8 KJV).

The apostle Paul affirms this, stating, "(For the weapons of our warfare are not carnal, but mighty through God to the pulling down of strong holds;) casting down imaginations, and every high thing that exalteth itself against the knowledge of God, and bringing into captivity every thought to the obedience of Christ" (2 Corinthians 10:4–5 KJV).

We must become spiritually mature, recognizing that Jesus came to destroy the works of the devil not on the outside of us, but on the inside. For this purpose, the Lord gives us His spirit, who through great patience, love, and grace, purges the garrisons the devil may have set up within us. He sets us free from the bondage of bitterness and lack of forgiveness.

The health of our soul is tremendously affected by how we respond to offense! In fact, even our physical health is affected by the toxic spiritual spillovers we harbor within us through unforgiveness, spreading the toxicity over a multitude of areas in our lives.

Without diving too deep into statistics, medical discoveries have identified a link between heart disease, cholesterol levels, stress, anxiety, and various conditions that are linked with unforgiveness. They finally caught up with what God has been telling people in His Word for thousands of years!

God is not just incredible, His Word is absolutely credible, especially regarding forgiveness! It's imperative to forgive, not only for the sake of the one who brought the offense, but for you who is harboring it. We are unauthorized, by God's divine law, to harbor spiritual fugitives such as lust, love of money, murder, or whatever is not welcome in the home of our heart. If we are caught, there will be consequences. Therefore, when we stand before God, we need to stand before Him without any fugitives hiding in our heart. One of these fugitives is self-righteousness.

Pious self-exaltation occurs when we engage in frequent discussions about Jesus and have less discussions with Him. Unwillingness to forgive is blatant hypocrisy. It pushes others down, while pulling the ego up. However, this duality is quite intriguing since it reveals who is actually afflicted in soul. When we behave self-righteously, we magnify the sins of others against us, but cloak the heap of the sins we've committed against God. This adds an often indiscernible weight to our soul. No wonder our entire being is crying out for liberation!

CHAPTER 5

Permissible Versus Beneficial

> Everything is permissible, but not everything is beneficial. Everything is permissible, but not everything is edifying. (1 Corinthians 10:23 BSB)

Let me start by saying that sin—anything that is offensive to God—is absolutely not permissible or beneficial. In fact, it's quite the opposite—destructive and harmful. Therefore, let us not abuse this scripture and the wisdom Jesus provides us through it. This passage is written with the heart of not offending those around us, but to seek the best for their well-being, as we would for ourselves, for in this way we will be pleasing before God and others.

This is contrary to the selfish nature of sin, which exclaims that "it's all about you." Digging deeper into the advice given to us by these precious words, we must be careful in the making of our decisions. Our decisions reveal many things about our character, whether we are inclined to believe it or not. Paramount to the success of our soul is not simply revelation of our true character, but to thwart any attempt of falsely vouching for ourselves, only to unwittingly detriment our souls in the spectrum of time. Either way, we must make decisions with the understanding that our decisions eventually make us.

What I mean by this last statement of "our decisions make us" is simple. We become what we do! You can only repeat an action frequently enough until it becomes a part of your character. For example, if I properly and consistently work out my body, then I will be fit because I am exercising on a regular basis. I, therefore, have made a beneficial decision which will enhance my health. In the same light, if I make the decision to remain lazy and give in to my tiredness, then my health will degenerate over a period of time and can, in worst-case scenarios, lead me to permanent health deficiencies or even death.

Now let's examine the last line of this scripture with greater depth, "but not everything is edifying." Our decisions are of utmost importance because they usually affect those around us, even without our knowledge. If I am a smoker and smoke around others, I am ultimately forcing them to secondhand smoke and therefore affecting their health, as well as my own.

Obviously, I know that smoking is an unhealthy habit that often turns into an addiction and causes great harm and suffering. In fact, my habit can potentially cause cancer in my body and then cause emotional, mental, and financial suffering for those around me. Although it is legal and in a way permissible to do, it is absolutely and without a doubt *not* edifying to those within my reach.

Am I condemning smokers? Absolutely not! However, I am unapologetically condemning smoking as an action that is harmful to both the user and those within proximity. In fact, I have family members that have smoked and quit, yet I have others who remain smokers. I have friends that are having open-heart surgery due to respiratory complications from smoking, and yet I love them all, without shaming them. This hurts their families deeply and therefore proves that just because you are free to do something, even if governments allow for it, does not make it something worth engaging in.

The Golden Rule

Let us add unto this knowledge the golden rule: "Do to others as you would have them do to you" (Luke 6:31 NIV).

If we truly keep this in mind, our decisions will not only be of the highest ethical standards, but will help us to create highly effective habits that create highly effective character. These decisions will keep our souls healthy and free from the bondage that comes with sinful behavior. If we apply this rule with integrity, we will safeguard our own hearts, proving the benefits of our decisions. The proper decisions we make reflect the heart of God so beautifully, causing others to see that Jesus is truly alive in us.

Choices made in love and selflessness will produce these results. However, choices selected in selfishness will produce that which Jesus is constantly delivering us from…ourselves. We must think with the potential end result in mind before we take action. If you are someone who has admittedly been on the road of terrible decisions and hate yourself for it, please know that you still have opportunity to change that which is in your control, leaving the rest up to Jesus. None of us can do this on our own or in our own strength. Hating yourself will never enable you to live the fullness of the life God has given you.

Often, people are sick without knowledge of how to heal from their illness. In order to heal, the issue first needs to be identified. In the same way, internalize the truth that Jesus presents in His Word and use the tactics illustrated through this book to take proper measures in applying some of the tools that will help heal and prosper your soul.

Freedom Within Boundaries

If you've never watched Disney's *The Lion King* (1994, 2D edition), what in the world have you been doing? I'm just kidding, but seriously go and watch it! Nostalgia just set in for the '90s babies like me! For those who have seen this incredible film, you may remember a scene where Mufasa is conversing with Simba about his future reign as king of Pride Rock, exhorting him to avoid the shadowy places that border their kingdom. However, Simba's folly, led by his ambition to one day be king, pushes him into danger, where his father must rescue him from the dark because he overestimated the bounds of his freedom.

Oh, what great love God has for His people, that He would hide such powerful truths in a children's film for His people to grasp; what wisdom, carried through the vehicle of these words, between two fictitious lions conversing!

Wisdom in Liberty

You see, in a nutshell, Mufasa was teaching Simba not to abuse his freedom as a future king. He was teaching him that there is also a kingdom of darkness that will hinder the kingdom of light and to remain walking in the light. In this way, the darkness could not reach him. What a powerful illustration that parallels our lives!

> For, brethren, ye have been called unto liberty; only use not liberty for an occasion to the flesh, but by love serve one another. For all the law is fulfilled in one word, even in this; Thou shalt love thy neighbour as thyself. But if ye bite and devour one another, take heed that ye be not consumed one of another. This I say then, "Walk in the Spirit, and ye shall not fulfil the lust of the flesh." (Galatians 5:13–16 KJV)

> It is for freedom that Christ has set us free. Stand firm, then, and do not let yourselves be burdened again by a yoke of slavery. (Galatians 5:1 NIV)

It is nothing short of amazing to know that our Heavenly Father has called us unto freedom, that Jesus died in our place to give us freedom, that the Holy Ghost empowers us to live out that freedom and, in turn, to help set others free. However, in all of this, God has placed necessary limitations in our lives for the very sake of remaining free.

As Simba was instructed on how to use his freedom wisely, so the Lord, our Father, also desires that we use the freedom given to us wisely. We are not to even go near the "shadowy place." How brilliant! God wants to keep us away from the kingdom of darkness because we do not belong to it, although we may have at one point! Look at what His Word says: "But ye are a chosen generation, a royal priesthood, an holy nation, a peculiar people; that ye should shew forth the praises of him who hath called you out of darkness into his marvelous light" (1 Peter 2:9 KJV).

God has called us out of something, but also into something! We are called into His kingdom—His marvelous light! Why then would we revert to a place of sin, with the liberty afforded to us by the blood of Jesus? He calls us kings and priests of the kingdom of light! Again expressing that "The Spirit Himself bears witness with our spirit that we are children of God, and if children, then heirs—heirs of God and joint heirs with Christ, if indeed we suffer with Him, that we may also be glorified together" (Romans 8:16–17 KJV).

It is therefore in our best interest to choose things that benefit the King and the kingdom we belong to, for we ourselves are heirs of it. We must take keen acknowledgment of our words, actions, and endeavors, ensuring that we don't squander the precious cost of our liberty—the body and blood of Jesus. Although permissibility is not talking about sin (for then it would be impermissible), I took the *liberty* to express these statements regarding freedom because the downside to permissible can indeed lead to bondage, baited by sin. If you struggle to remember, think of it as such: Permissible is good; beneficial is great. Aim to lay down that which is good to lay hold of that which is great, even when harder to do so. The results will speak for themselves.

CHAPTER 6

Convictions and Confessions

There are two C's to remember in this chapter that will help keep immense weight off of your soul: *conviction* and *confession*. Although in the context which I speak of them, they differ from one another, these two C's are advantageous to the health of your person.

Conviction may be defined as follows: 1) finding a criminal guilty of a crime in a court of law; 2) a deeply held belief, opinion, or standard; 3) to be persuaded of something, convinced.

It is cardinal to understand that conviction is simply the driving force behind why we do the things we do. This chapter is focused solely on definition 2 and 3 of conviction. Furthermore, true conviction reaches into the deepest parts of a person's soul and often involves the intersecting of the mind, will, emotions, and conscience.

Since we've defined conviction, it's of great importance to define confession. Now, confession is not only a formal tradition of the Catholic Church, where a member confides in the priest about something weighing on their heart, followed by intercessory prayers for that specified and confidential matter.

Confession, in my own words, is anything that one may need to admit, which may be expressed in confidentiality or publicly as the nature of the situation merits.

With these understandings defined, let's use definition 2 and 3 of conviction and let's use my definition of confession to better understand how these two C's work hand in hand in the prospering of the soul.

These Are My Confessions

Yes, the above subheading is indeed an Usher reference—moving on now! When I was in my young twenties, I was engaged to a woman I thought I would marry. I was so convinced in fact, that I ignored every red flag and bulldozed through all the opposition that I later understood was actually beneficial counsel. When God called me away from that relationship because of its extreme toxicity (on both ends), it started with a simple instruction. The instruction grew to an understanding, which later became something I believed. Following belief, it became a conviction that this relationship was unhealthy and had to end. I wrestled with my conviction to stay in the relationship out of love and duty to my fiancée, so much so, that after I called it off once, I asked her to marry me a second time. Yes, engaged to the same woman twice!

I put her through hell twice because I truly believed that we could make something work when the Holy Spirit had already convicted me on numerous occasions, in various ways, that this was not His will. Fear, guilt, shame, lust, and a very toxic version of what we thought was love kept us together. As I intentionally procrastinated the will of God and continually hardened my heart to the conviction of the Holy Ghost, the weight of sin on my soul grew heavier and heavier. It got to the point where my physical body began to suffer and I felt forced to confess how I was honestly feeling.

After confessing, I was compelled to act upon my conviction with the understanding that confession without action is empty. It's like when the person who cheats in the relationship confesses and apologizes, but then goes right back to cheating. No one cares for that confession unless it's accompanied by a repentant action. That repentant action is fueled by conviction.

Let me not fail to mention the deceptive act of a half-hearted confession. These types of confessions are an ensnarement to the soul which has imagined that shortcuts come with no cost. A true confession must be wholly stated and honest in nature or else it simply becomes partially revealed deceit. A classic example involves teens that speak ill of their parents' behavior toward them, but fail to disclose that their parents actions were actually a reaction to their misconduct.

Partial confessions are not reliable. In actuality, they dismantle integrity and credibility. It may appear as if they have an advantage over others who choose to remain silent, given an opportunity to admit something; however, this places the confessor in a tense situation. The immediate issue at hand is the illusion of resolution. In truth, there are strings attached from the secretive issue to future events that will take on the nature of a land mine. As soon as the guilty party steps into the wrong space…an explosive of confession will more than likely occur, instead of a risky, but gentle, dismantling of the situation at hand. Not to mention that an emotional explosion makes way for an emotional implosion. Information suppressed must eventually be expressed for freedom of the soul, from the weight of guilt.

Don't Harden Your Heart

In the life of a Christian, the conviction of the Holy Ghost cannot be taken lightly. There are severe implications when ignoring the words God communicates to us generally through His Word and specifically through various means such as people, dreams, visions, inward compelling convictions, and various avenues.

> Today, if you will hear His voice, do not harden your hearts as in the rebellion. (Hebrews 3:15 NKJV)

> For he doth not afflict willingly nor grieve the children of men. (Lamentations 3:33 KJV)

When coupling these verses, you get a great understanding for the heart of God. Our Heavenly Father convicts for our good, not to harm us. We, however, walk in the schemes of our deceptive hearts, and therefore, God steps in to save us from unnecessary traumas that we may cause ourselves.

Does this sound familiar to some of you? If you've ever received the "gut feeling" and followed through with what it was indicating, you've probably experienced the Lord convicting you for your own good. We, however, ignorantly rob God of His glory when we remove Him from the picture and emphasize that our gut had a mind of its own, acting on pure untraceable intuition. How about the "I-heard-a-small-voice" or "felt-like-someone-told-me" expressions? The faith drawn out by conviction empowers us to move into or away from something beneficial or damaging to our soul. We must remain in a posture of obedience for the sake of our soul.

The Saving Power of Confession

Frequently, Christians, especially those new to the faith, are convicted to confess to their friends that they can no longer live the same way after having met Jesus. Confession is extremely powerful, insomuch that the Word of God teaches that in order to start our walk with God, the first step is a confession.

> That if thou shalt confess with thy mouth the Lord Jesus, and shalt believe in thine heart that God hath raised him from the dead, thou shalt be saved. (Romans 10:9 KJV)

In our journey with God, we will have times where we fail to live according to the Lord's standards and need to confess our sin before Him, in order to receive the ongoing forgiveness He offers us through the blood of Jesus.

> If we confess our sins, he is faithful and just to forgive us our sins, and to cleanse

us from all unrighteousness. (1 John 1:9 KJV)

Confession opens the floodgates of forgiveness! Moreover, the Word of God teaches us to "confess your faults one to another, and pray one for another, that ye may be healed. The effectual fervent prayer of a righteous man availeth much" (James 5:16 KJV).

Therefore, confessing before God provides us with forgiveness and confessing to the people of God brings us healing. These two confessions, driven by conviction, help us to prosper our souls. It's so wonderful to think that God has disclosed a piece of His nature in the system of confession. Read for yourself below:

> For the perverse person is an abomination to the LORD, but His secret counsel is with the upright. (Proverbs 3:32 NKJV)

In this simple passage, King Solomon speaks to the nature of God confiding in the righteous. Yes, God confides in man! Here's another one: "The secret of the Lord is with them that fear him; and he will shew them his covenant" (Psalm 25:14 KJV).

Every time we confess or confide in the Lord or His people, we practice His nature. It's no wonder why the devil aims to keep us from doing so by using tactics of shame, guilt, and condemnation.

For these reasons, don't let fear undermine the power of confession and bully you into making them half-hearted. Some weight can only be dropped through this amazing system that God created to make sure His people thrive internally. You need to know that it's okay to make mistakes! It's okay not to have it all together. It's okay to have room to grow and improve. None of us have yet arrived or attained perfection. It's an amazing thing to know that a perfect God is in love with His imperfect people! It's His love that compels us to walk out what the Holy Spirit is continually producing internally. God draws out what has anchored itself in the dark, not for the sake of exposing us to shame, but for our healing and benefit.

When Adam and Eve sinned in the garden of Eden, they ran away from God, instead of to Him. God did not turn away from them! They proceeded to hide from God behind strung-together fig leaves—their best attempt to cover their unrighteousness. God still met them in the midst of their sin and shame, exposed the problem, and brought upon them, the earth and Satan, the consequences due them. He then covered them with the skin of an animal, which contains prophetic undertones that Jesus, the Lamb of God, would one day cover the world's mistakes with His righteousness.

The system of sacrificing animals continued until Jesus arrived on the earth as a man, took up the cross, died for our sins, and rose again (in the flesh) on the third day, ascending back to the Father after forty days. Perfect love runs toward us in our brokenness, not away! Take note: The nature of sin is to isolate us from God, tactfully shaming us away from our source of help. The first step back toward God is turning your heart toward Him in repentance (internal). Step two manifests what is on the inside with an outward confession (both to God and to people). Step three is continuing to honor God with the lifestyle that accompanies repentance. The sooner we run to Him, the sooner we run toward freedom. We are incapable of lifting the heavy burden of secret sin for long periods of time before it begins to crush us. Repent, confess, get free. Now is the time.

CHAPTER 7

Rest and Sleep

I couldn't quite possibly think of a more appropriate chapter to include this important element in causing your soul to prosper than in chapter 7.

> And on the seventh day God ended his work which he had made; and he rested on the seventh day from all his work which he had made. And God blessed the seventh day, and sanctified it: because that in it he had rested from all his work which God created and made. (Genesis 2:2–3 KJV)

Wait a second, buddy… God…rest…huh? Have you ever pondered the idea of Almighty God having to raise His feet, while having one of the angels in heaven bring Him a heavenly beverage and telling all the saints, "I'm taking the day off. All prayers will be answered the next earth day!" No way! That's absurd! Let me prove it by scripture for argument's sake:

> Behold, he that keepeth Israel shall neither slumber nor sleep. (Psalm 121:4 KJV)

> Hast thou not known? hast thou not heard, that the everlasting God, the LORD, the Creator of the ends of the earth, fainteth not, neither is weary? there is no searching of his understanding. (Isaiah 40:28 KJV)

So why did God rest on the seventh day? He did this to set an example for mankind, having the superior method in maintaining a healthy creation as a master craftsman and creator. Some workaholics may be hating this part of the book right now, but I promise it is in your best interest!

The essential importance of rest cannot be replaced, ignored, or neglected if you truly want to see your soul become healthy. Rest is a safeguard for your body, soul, and spirit. It is recommended to take one full day of rest... by God, and science agrees with God, so it's something we must prioritize for our overall health, capiche? Rest is not a heart-wrenching rule to penalize you for your great accomplishments throughout the week. It is not a kind of quarantine on your life's schedule! In fact, it's a reward for those who have, in a sense, earned it, and it is to be appreciated, not dreaded. Rest is so serious that God included it in His top ten commandments! Wait a second...in fact, it actually made top five!

If you're anything like me, you either need to be completely in motion, or completely resting, but avoiding the great chasm that lies somewhere in between. The in-between encapsulates anxiety, birthed by uncertainty because you know things need to get done, but continue contemplating all the factors regarding the how, when, what-ifs, etc. If that's you, good news! There's hope! A simple step I take to organize my mental loads often includes writing out a list and scratching things off, usually starting with the thing I feel needs my attention immediately, until I reach what requires the least of my attention. In this way, I make sure to hit my goals for the day frequently and I'm reminded of what I *must* accomplish.

However, in the midst of the busy, I've come to learn that rest is a holy and sacred space. This time is a gift that is given to us in order to effectively reflect, refresh, and reconnect with Jesus. Now some of you may think rest equals literally doing nothing and staring at a wall. That's absolutely not true! Let's break down the walls of confusion and free you from your agonizing fear of rest by simply stating what rest is not, versus, what it actually is.

Rest Is Not

Below are a few ideas and concepts debunking myths behind rest. Rest is not:

1) Physically working out on your day off. Even athletes know that for your muscles to repair properly, they need a break time. Working out includes outdoor activities too…no cheating!

2) Doing more work. Just because you are not getting paid for it does not mean that it is not work. Many have deceived themselves in claiming that household chores do not constitute work. Some overexert themselves in doing more work on their days off, rather than during their work-week schedules. This can magnetize mental, emotional, and physical strain.
3) Cooking every meal, unless you absolutely have to. Have leftovers for a day, it won't kill you.
4) Breaking your bank? Have you considered taking a day to save money, not spend it. A mini-secret to making it last longer.
5) Doing the same things you would usually do in a reduced amount. Just stop already!
6) Rest is not sleep. One can be terribly restless during sleep.

Before we continue, let me be absolutely crystal clear on the obvious. Rest is not a scapegoat from your responsibilities. Now repeat that sentence slowly a few times, making sure it hits your body, soul, and spirit. I'm kidding! If you actually did that, kudos to you! You get bonus points!

Now, since we've defined what rest is not, let's explore what it is. Rest is:

1.) a cessation of work or motion in order to replenish strength;
2.) to remain in a specific place or positioning;
3.) the halting of any extraneous activity; and
4.) silence over a period of time.

Interestingly enough, it seems that in order to rest, we must actively engage ourselves in doing so. Therefore, *resting is an active activity*. It may start off with difficulty, but as we invest in the discipline of rest, it will pay out great dividends when adequately applied.

How to Practice Rest

1) Schedule work and rest. Write rest into your schedule. Aim for a full twenty-four-hour rest period, one day a week, with minor breaks daily.
2) Taking a light walk alone to pray, think, or enjoy a particular view, or perhaps with a loved one, friends, etc. *Light* does not mean start training for a marathon.
3) On your rest day, don't go around meeting the wants of another, but instead, meet only *needs*. You can't recharge while making sure everyone is refueled but yourself.
4) *Selah*. This powerful word found frequently in the book of Psalms is a Hebrew word meaning pause, break, end, or rest. After a psalm where this word is inserted, it is intended to cause us to reflect on what was being sung unto God. How can we apply it? Think of your week and look to see what God did, what He spoke. It's often in our reflection where revelation is distributed for all we missed in our busyness. It's a place where vision is cultivated and strengthened.
5) Watching a godly film/God-approved movie. Let me be real with you; there's a lot of trash on the big screen, but simply asking Jesus to watch with you and to speak to you through what you're watching

creates intimacy in the rest. Watch something you know Jesus would be okay watching based on His Word. Don't watch things filled with witchcraft, blasphemy of God, fornication, cussing, etc. It may be difficult to find, but there is a lot of good media to consume. Like healthier foods, it may take longer to find and cost more time, but the positive effects on your soul will be worth it.

6) Being > Doing. Sometimes you need to be in the moment, not do more to make that moment better. Rest requires you to be > do.

Rest Is for the Laborer

If you've been eating this book up, maybe you should take a break and rest...again. Kidding, unless you're exhausted...then I am not. Go do what you gotta do and come back in a few!

Now that we have a few examples of what rest is and is not, we need to know who it is for. Rest and laziness are not the same, although they sometimes have similar characteristics in a short-term scope. In addition, rest and sleep differ in nature from one another, even when they can simultaneously coexist. Often nightmares are the proof; one is asleep, but not resting, only to be awakened in a state of anxiety, fear, or confusion. Although their body may be rested, their psyche is waring for rest.

Jesus says, "Come unto me, all ye that labour and are heavy laden, and I will give you rest. Take my yoke upon you, and learn of me; for I am meek and lowly in heart: and ye shall find rest unto your souls. For my yoke is easy, and my burden is light" (Matthew 11:28–30 KJV).

It's quite fascinating that Jesus is speaking to a specific audience here. He's not talking to those who are lazy or rested. He's talking to those that labor, to those who are wearied by life and exhausted in whatever sense that may be! He's talking to you and I! When we labor and get tired, He is the rest that we need!

The issue is that we never genuinely accept the invitation of that rest because we aim to attain it for ourselves by doing more, instead of letting God work on our behalf! Have you forgotten that when we rest, God moves the mountains we never could! When we rest, we are trusting God with our time and submitting to His schedule, which includes a day of rest! Resting in Jesus is a trust thing! Do we trust Him with our schedule? Do we truly trust that God knows what we need to do more than we do?

I love this famous quote by Martin Luther: "I have so much to do that I shall spend the first three hours in prayer."

When I first heard it, I was taken back. I was thinking something along the lines of "Are you serious? You mean to tell me that you spend more time with God when you have more to do?" Yes! We need to spend more time resting in Jesus, with Jesus! It's so unnatural to our nature, but the more we do this, the more God can do through us! It boggles my mind how we tend to understand this concept with everything around us and yet have difficulty applying it to ourselves.

Our cellphone batteries need to charge, our pets need a break, our cars need gas refilled, etc. As we see around us, God is continuously showing us that we have limits, and knowing our limits leads us to depend on He who is limitless. Praise be to Jesus!

Catching Some Z's

Sleep gives night life a whole new meaning! God designed us in such a way for our body, mind, and soul to be active during our sleep. So think with me. If we are made in God's image, then what a simply profound revelation it is to know that God is at work while we sleep. Here are four facts regarding sleep:

1) *Mental secretary.* Our brain processes information from the day and compartmentalizes them as we sleep. This aids in building long-term memory.
2) *Healing and hormones.* When one is sick, has undergone surgery, or is exhausted from strenuous physical labor, one of the recommendations commonly given is to sleep and rest for adequate and elongated periods of time, until recovery has taken place. Hormones distributed throughout the body as we sleep are released to help our bodies heal, grow, and replenish our strength.
3) *Healthy attitude linked to quality sleep.* Sometimes it's not so spiritual as it is physical. Lack of quality sleep is often linked to a lack of quality attitude. Getting snappy, angry, sensitive? Maybe you just need a nap. If this problem persists, sleep is not the culprit behind your unpleasant disposition.

4) *Dreams.* Dreams reveal that either God is speaking or that our minds are working through what they are aiming to process. See the scriptures below:

> As a dream comes through many cares. (Ecclesiastes 5:3 BSB)

> In a dream, in a vision of the night, when deep sleep falleth upon men, in slumberings upon the bed; Then he openeth the ears of men, and sealeth their instruction. (Job 33:15–16 KJV)

Wisdom expresses that we should not expect more of ourselves than God does. It's okay to take breaks—to rest and sleep—and to rest in our sleep. God made us to recharge and modeled for us this powerful truth when He Himself rested. Again, the reason being for us: "And He said to them, 'The Sabbath was made for man, and not man for the Sabbath'" (Mark 2:27 NKJV).

Many know that when His precious friend Lazarus died, *Jesus wept.* However, we fail to recognize that *Jesus slept*: "And, behold, there arose a great tempest in the sea, insomuch that the ship was covered with the waves: but he was asleep" (Matthew 8:24 KJV).

It sounds so elementary, but continuously we tend to combat ourselves when all we need is to simply give ourselves permission to be human. In this digital age, we are often duped into functioning like a robot, aiming to produce results as if we are one. God made us human; sometimes we have to fight with our schedules to stay that way.

How Serious Is It?

Continual lack of sleep can lead to shorter lifespans. In some cases, an excess amount of sleep can cause health issues as well. The point is, don't default to either extreme. Nothing is worth your life. Your health can unsuspectingly be a ticking time bomb, immersed in habit.

Let's not forget that God gave us a twenty-four-hour day. If we are to adequately sleep, that makes up about one-third of our day, which conclusively affects one-third of our lives! Sleep affects everything!

Many are familiar with the satirical stereotype of the grouchy grandpa or the grumpy grandma. However, sleep deprivation can actually be far more life-threatening than we understand it to be. Sleepy drivers pose a similar risk to that of a drunk driver. When a person is deprived of their natural recharging process, the effects can be as simple as annoyance in the short term, but detrimental in the long term. I've personally had several friends fall asleep at the wheel as they've totaled their cars, surviving only by the grace of God. Sleep and rest are imperative in protecting a person and those surrounding them from great unintended harm.

Social Sleepiness

Social Scenario #1

Thirsting for sleep or rest is often expressed in what scholars and great thinkers call—are you ready for it—*the yawn*. Have you ever been engaged in business meeting, only to realize that your body is present but your mind disappeared at some point in time, yet you continue to nod, affirm, and agree with important information that fails to register in your memory? To make matters worse, you get ambushed by...*the yawn*, only to have a slow-motion replay in your mind of your boss' reaction, who now knows without a doubt you've been checked out for the past fifteen minutes! This is followed by an awkward two seconds of silence. Just as you're about to get reprimanded in front of your colleagues, *the yawn* is now reciprocated, and miraculously, you're able to recall specific points of conversation in the time your boss yawns and the time you are asked to answer his question. You're off the hook! Barely escaped!

Social Scenario #2

You're on a first date and you want to make a good impression. You really desire for the person to know that you are hanging on their every word. You're deeply focused and immersed in the pleasant conversation, only to be interrupted by...*the yawn*. Now you notice the other person trying to wrap up the conversation because of their misperceived disinterest on your part. What a mess!

Although it's usually not as dramatized as I've painted some of these scenarios to be, our social lives are impacted by sleep deprivation. For these reasons, rest and sleep are socially important as well. Furthermore, a good night's rest—again, not to be conjoined with our understanding of sleep—rejuvenates the body and allows the brain to be engaged at its optimal level. For this purpose, make certain you are not living a lifestyle on fumes. Eventually your engine will burn out and the damage may be irreversible. God wants us well rested: "It is vain for you to rise up early, to sit up late, to eat the bread of sorrows: for so he giveth his beloved sleep" (Psalm 127:2 KJV).

CHAPTER 8

Spiritual Anatomy

Everyone who has a high school experience expresses personal stories that embody their particular experiences. Some of these stories are academic, relational, and even deeply personal. However, there's one thing every high school student has in common. They have to take an assortment of classes and score well enough to pass these classes. If not, they are at risk of failing. With enough failed classes, a student may fail an entire grade and have to repeat it until they meet the qualifications to pass.

I remember a specific semester in high school in which I received my report card. I was working my tail off at the time and aiming to get the best possible grades I could. Upon opening the mail (I know we can now look things up online, but this was a while ago); I was a little taken back. I was in disbelief as I reviewed the six letters going down the card. They read as follows: A, A, A…another A, A, and a giant *F* in math. Speaking of math, something wasn't adding up! At this point I may have been so excited that I scored 5 A's for the semester that the letter "F in my mind stood for "fantastic."

After great deliberation and masterful deducing, I came to the astounding conclusion that I was utterly failing my class!

I was giving math my best shot, but it subtracted my efforts, multiplied my sorrows, divided my mind, and at this point I would have been content with a pie, but not this kind: π. It was only Algebra II! I was beginning to discern that my *best* was simply not good enough! The celebration of A's was offset with the giant F, and if there was even the slightest doubt in my parents' minds as to whether I was giving school an honest effort, this report card was it. As a family, we knew that I needed help to decipher this hieroglyphic language called "mathematics" in it's multitude of incarnations!

It's at this point in time that we began to intentionally look for the appropriate help, in hopes of adjusting that F to a more visually appealing letter. This problem probed me to look outside of myself; therefore, I went to what was immediately available—my parents. Although my parents were excellent in teaching me other things, the level of math I was undertaking required somewhat of a veteran in this arena. Therefore, I endeavored to search for a plausible alternative.

Now, I had a wonderful Nigerian math teacher (let's call him Mr. A) whom I befriended and became very close to. I remember spending elongated amounts of time taking notes as I sat at my desk, in an empty classroom after school, during lunch and on my fifteen-minute breaks. I would fasten my eyes on him as he wrote on the black chalkboard, which spanned the front of the classroom, much like a giant TV screen. As he would helpfully dictate and explain the same formulaic solutions to simple problems numerous times, my mind began to grasp bits of information.

I knew this man had to know God because of his great patience with me, since he always treated me with kindness and tended to my academic needs, aware that I was genuinely wrestling with equations and formulas that my mind could not comprehend. You know that phrase people say, "My brain hurts?" Well, mine often did, yet his explanations of the mathematical universe repeatedly eased my distressed mind.

After being seated under his tutelage for countless hours, I began retaining enough understanding of the subject matter to obtain a C by the semester's end.

More Than Math

As excited as everyone is to hear about my high school math journey to less than average success, this chapter would be wasted if that's all we talked about. In fact, this story was intended to lead to a subject that the Lord Jesus is deeply passionate about—His church! His body! His bride! This vast and innumerable network of sons and daughters, each equipped with a unique purpose for the edification of their spiritual siblings and for the glorification of God.

> And He Himself gave some to be apostles, some prophets, some evangelists, and some pastors and teachers, for the equipping of the saints for the work of ministry, for the edifying of the body of Christ, till we all come to the unity of the faith and of the knowledge of the Son of God, to a perfect man, to the measure of the stature of the fullness of Christ; that

> we should no longer be children, tossed to and fro and carried about with every wind of doctrine, by the trickery of men, in the cunning craftiness of deceitful plotting, but, speaking the truth in love, may grow up in all things into Him who is the head—Christ—from whom the whole body, joined and knit together by what every joint supplies, according to the effective working by which every part does its share, causes growth of the body for the edifying of itself in love. (Ephesians 4:11–16 NKJV)

Jesus has selected us! Yes, you and I! He has chosen us to be knit together as one body, a Jesus people! Just like the body is built up piece by piece, bone by bone, muscle by muscle, tissue by tissue, and cell by cell, there is absolutely no way we can diminish the importance of how every part of our spiritual body is essential. No one in their right mind will intentionally harm themselves and cut off pieces of their physical body. There is no logical sense or gain in performing such harmful acts. So how is it that we think we benefit from cutting off people in the church?

As obvious as the above fact seems (physically), we tend to do this in the spiritual sense all the time, and I believe it's of paramount importance to discuss how to properly function in the body, to learn how to function alongside of the community that you are called into. After all, heaven gave the mandate. Yet in all this, know that I am not taking into account those who bring disease to the body and ultimately harm it.

Stay Connected

One of the wonderful reasons that our Heavenly Father created us with limitations is to network with other members of the church, which can help us in our time of need. For example, if I know someone who ministers healing and I need a miracle due to an illness, disease, or physical disability, I should intentionally seek out my brother or sister after I've sought the Lord. They may be the conduits which God has intended to use in facilitating my healing. Moreover, if the Lord has grown me in a prophetic gifting and a brother or sister needs a word of knowledge, affirmation, direction, or exhortation from the Lord, they should seek me out after seeking God first, because I am called to equip them.

The Lord wants to use His body, for His body, until we all come to unity in Jesus, as one. It sounds rudimentary, but we tend to overcomplicate the matter. If you are oblivious to this fact, I'd like clarify something: The body of Christ, aka the church, is so diverse in nature, and this is the way God has called it to be. His bride is pleasing to Him with her different sexes, ages, races, cultures, nations, languages, geographical locations, biblical traditions, ceremonies, gifting, ministries, forms of worship, etc. God Himself is diverse. Hello! The Trinity! The one we call Provider, Teacher, Healer, Savior, Friend, Shepherd, and so much more! Do you get the picture?

Regarding differences in giftings, administrations, operations, and manifestations of the Holy Ghost, given for the sake of benefiting the body as a whole, please take a moment to pause and read 1 Corinthians 12.

As we continue seeking the Lord, be open to His leading to connect with other body parts! Many times over, He has placed the answer to their prayers within you and the answers to your prayers within them. God has chosen to manifest Himself in each of the members of His church's lives differently for the benefit of all. The Lord Jesus reveals this desire in several scriptures.

Take Acts 9 as a template. Jesus shows up, blinds and impedes the travels of the apostle Paul (also known as Saul of Tarsus), who, at that time, is known for murdering Christians.

Jesus then uses other members of the body to minister to this man, especially while he remains blind for three days. This man of wickedness later becomes one of the greatest men to have ever walked the earth for the glory of God.

For these purposes, let's grow in the maturity not to cut off those who are less appealing to society, those who are broken, and those who are poor. Let us love these body parts back to health and integrate them into God's wonderful plans and destinies for their lives. The person you despise today may be the person you need tomorrow. Raise them up in Jesus name, not only looking on their present condition or circumstances, but on their created value.

The Devil's Plan for Division

Many of us have fallen prey to the lies of the devil, which, when believed, are intended to extract us from the body of Christ into isolation, often through offense, conditioning our souls to gaze at petty differences instead of the depth of our similarities. Are we so blind to the demonic strategies here?

Look at what the apostle Paul says: "Now whom you forgive anything, I also forgive. For if indeed I have forgiven anything, I have forgiven that one for your sakes in the presence of Christ, lest Satan should take advantage of us; for we are not ignorant of his devices" (2 Corinthians 2:11–12 NKJV).

Satan's goal is exposed in John 10:10—to *kill, steal,* and *destroy*—but he also comes to *divide.* Jesus reveals something imperative for us to grasp if we want our souls to prosper in the below scripture.

> But Jesus knew their thoughts, and said to them: "Every kingdom divided against itself is brought to desolation, and every city or house divided against itself will not stand." (Matthew 12:25 NKJV)

In fact, the Word of God commands us not to divide, provided things are healthy and in order.

> And let us consider one another to provoke unto love and to good works: Not forsaking the assembling of ourselves together, as the manner of some is; but exhorting one another: and so much the more, as ye see the day approaching. (Hebrews 10:25 KJV)

We are called to add and multiply, as we continue to serve one another in unity and love. Again, this is not in reference to unhealthy things in the body that must be dealt with. Therefore, we must make informed, mature, and truthful decisions, with perennial examination of our motives in regards to befriending someone or distancing ourselves from them altogether.

Who Is the Body of Christ?

The body of Christ is exclusive to Him in the same way that our physical bodies are exclusive to us. I cannot live inside of another body, neither can the Holy Ghost dwell in those who have not received Jesus as Lord. Now, Jesus gives us a model to determine who "the body" is: "For whosoever shall do the will of my Father which is in heaven, the same is my brother, and sister, and mother" (Matthew 12:50 KJV).

If that was His standard, it must become our standard. Not everyone that goes to a church building is truly a part of the body, and not everyone who is absent of the congregation is cut off. Not everyone who calls Jesus "Lord" truly walks with Him. Therefore, we must cautiously, prayerfully, and wisely pick them which we give a voice into our lives.

In the same way that we have understanding of healthy versus junk food, it is important to apply this concept to the spiritual body of Christ also. We cannot give credence to deceiving ourselves when the Holy Ghost makes a judgment upon something or someone.

> Woe unto them that call evil good, and good evil; that put darkness for light, and light for darkness; that put bitter for sweet, and sweet for bitter! (Isaiah 5:20 KJV)

Contrary to popular belief, not everyone belongs to God and not everyone belongs to the household of faith.

Here are a few scriptures to help us with this understanding as we seek God to build our communities:

> Beware of false prophets, which come to you in sheep's clothing, but inwardly they are ravening wolves. Ye shall know them by their fruits. Do men gather grapes of thorns, or figs of thistles? Even so every good tree bringeth forth good fruit; but a corrupt tree bringeth forth evil fruit. A good tree cannot bring forth evil fruit, neither can a corrupt tree bring forth good fruit. Every tree that bringeth not forth good fruit is hewn down, and cast into the fire. Wherefore by their fruits ye shall know them. (Matthew 7:15–20 KJV)

> As we have therefore opportunity, let us do good unto all men, especially unto them who are of the household of faith. (Galatians 6:10 KJV)

> He that committeth sin is of the devil; for the devil sinneth from the beginning. For this purpose the Son of God was manifested, that he might destroy the works of the devil. Whosoever is born of God doth not commit sin; for his seed remaineth in him: and he cannot sin, because he is born of God. In this the children of God are manifest, and the children of the devil: whosoever doeth not righteousness

> is not of God, neither he that loveth not his brother. (1 John 3:8–10 KJV)

It's of utmost importance not to edit the parts of the Holy Bible that we dislike adhering to. We must accept the Word of God as a whole in order to be whole. Some scriptures are indeed challenging, but they are there for our benefit, for the edification of others, and for the glory of King Jesus. Second Timothy 3:1–9 is another great example to learn from regarding who belongs to God or not.

Now regarding the subject of sin in the 1 John 3:8–10 passage, God is not condemning us when we sin. This scripture speaks of those who condemn themselves by remaining in willful sin, not to be confused by those who fall due to moments of weakness. Furthermore, this scripture does not grant license to condemn anyone, but instead, reveals who we belong to. Sin is of the devil; righteousness is of Jesus. We can't serve both. Plain and simple.

I've been the victim of choosing the wrong friendships because the name of Jesus was used as a password in which I was taken advantage of financially, spiritually, romantically, and many other "ly's." Please ask God who your friends should be and whom you should invest in. Love on sight, but trust slowly.

> Wounds from a friend can be trusted, but an enemy multiplies kisses. (Proverbs 27:6 NIV)

It's often the ones who call you out and stand up for truth—these are the ones you want to surround yourself with.

> Do not be deceived: "Evil company corrupts good habits." (1 Corinthians 15:33 NKJV)

I remember a specific relationship that God took issue with. During prayer one morning, I unexpectedly heard these words with extreme clarity: "The Holy Spirit has not given His approval of this woman for your life." It's important to note that He said, "your life." God did not call her wicked or evil, but revealed that she and I shared a troublesome toxicity, even before we were to be married, that would ultimately end in divorce. The combination would be problematic for the future God designed for us, with our differences being beyond reconciliation.

Please note that in the above paragraph we were unmarried. I caution those who are married not to apply the above concept to themselves, but if you find yourself drowning in marital troubles, seek God, counsel, and other healthy solutions to determine the appropriate steps forward.

Remember, even Jesus had His circle and did not spend all of His time with everybody. Therefore, whether someone is genuinely evil, not belonging to the family of God, or simply not beneficial your life, keep your soul healthy by not doing life with them. Release those whom God declares should not have access to you and don't chase if God removes them. Yet do not use this as an excuse to stay away from the right people! This includes those who disagree with you, those who present solutions for issues you don't desire to fix, those who are called to disciple you, and those who reveal truth even when you refuse to hear it, to name a few.

Patience With the Body

It is wise to keep in mind that the body matures over time, so don't be quick to judge those who do not yet appear to be on the level that *you* desire them to be on, erroneously cutting them off, when the Holy Spirit is sanctifying them. Use this understanding not to bypass serving your brothers and sisters in the Lord, who need your prayers and patience, but as you aim to disciple them, stand firm, receiving what you need from the Lord to remain fruitful.

Another quick tip to be cognizant of: Do not hold people to a standard that you yourself are unable to attain. That's hypocritical and a breach of your own integrity. Don't hold them higher than Jesus and don't hold them lower than you. This space in between the two keeps everyone healthy, just like our physical body is when we feed it properly.

> If it is possible, as much as depends on you, live peaceably with all men. (Romans 12:18 NKJV)

CHAPTER 9

Saying Yes Is Saying No

As we've delved into the conversation encompassing community and the importance of staying connected to the body of Christ, it is important to understand that you cannot give something that you do not have. Certainly, many times over, you've been asked to accommodate someone or something that you did not have the capacity to help. I want to make this point crystal clear: *That is completely okay.*

Imagine your car running on an empty gas tank or, for those of us who are a little fancier, running out of charge from the battery. The car would begin to show signs like engine sputter, power surges, etc. (for gas). These would indicate that the tank is running low and that your car needs to be refueled to carry out its proper functions. We are no different when it comes to the things of our body, our soul, and our spirit. If we don't have gas in the tank, we cannot prosper from within, while effectively helping others.

For someone to respond incredulously when you can't or are unable to provide something that they either want or need is in itself incredulous. To what standard would they hold you to if they themselves cannot contribute to the needs of another, due to their lack of abundance in a particular area? It is foolish for one to misjudge the intentions of another who cannot meet their demands. It is different entirely if they will not and indeed do have the means to supply what is needed. However, even in this, it is a case by case basis that is weighed based on the notion of "Should I meet this need? Why or why not?"

The Word We Must Learn to Use

> For do I now persuade men, or God? or do I seek to please men? for if I yet pleased men, I should not be the servant of Christ. (Galatians 1:10 KJV)

Have you ever been overwhelmed with your schedule and then created a plan to tackle each task one by one? Then somewhere along the line, someone asks you for a "favor" or they make their need known and place a weight on you through the most innocent of questions: "Can you please help me with _____?" Without their knowledge, you're already overwhelmed, but you have not communicated this to them. If you are a people pleaser, you will fall into the trap of becoming a *yes man*, someone who does or agrees with anything someone asks or tells them to do without hesitation.

The goal of a healthy soul should be to serve people, not to please them.

> For I do not mean that others should be eased and you burdened; but by an equality, that now at this time your abundance may supply their lack, that their abundance also may supply your lack—that there may be equality. As it is written, "He who gathered much had nothing left over, and he who gathered little had no lack." (2 Corinthians 8:13–15 NKJV)

Although this scripture is relating to monetary means and tangible resources, it also holds true for anything that you wish to supply, yet simply do not have. The intangible can encapsulate time, attention, strength, energy, affection, etc. This should not be taken lightly because the cost of neglecting yourself in areas of necessity long enough can bear dire consequence later. The apostle Paul advises us to give out of our abundance—that which is left over after our needs have been met.

Help You Help Them

If you've ever been on an airplane, you've probably experienced the airline's award-winning safety instructional videos (sarcasm). Somewhere during the video, we are led through what we should do if the cabin pressure changes. We are instructed to place the dropdown mask over our face properly and securely before assisting another in need. Those who've constructed these safety guidelines help make us aware that without helping ourselves, we will be of no use to those around us and can actually become a detriment in a state of emergency, instead of a help.

Therefore, we must be wise in the measure of help we give. Even Jesus Himself knew that He was called to serve one specific people group—Israel.

> But he answered and said, "I am not sent but unto the lost sheep of the house of Israel." (Matthew 15:24 KJV)

As a man, He was unable to be in multiple locations at one time and, therefore, unable to help everyone all at once. He often retreated to lonely and solitary places to pray because He knew that He needed the Father and the Holy Spirit's support in order to sustain His ministry. He knew that in order to help others, He first needed to be assisted by the Father and Holy Ghost. This was and is not due to lack of faith, instead it is simply an application of wisdom. To meet the needs of others, including the Gentiles, Jesus focused on raising up His immediate disciples who would, in turn, steward His church for generations to come. However, even they needed to delegate meeting the needs of others when the insurmountable pressures of a thriving church began to weigh them down.

> Now in these days when the disciples were increasing in number, a complaint by the Hellenists arose against the Hebrews because their widows were being neglected in the daily distribution. And the twelve summoned the full number of the disciples and said, "It is not right that we should give up preaching the word of God to serve tables. Therefore, brothers, pick out from among you seven men

of good repute, full of the Spirit and of wisdom, whom we will appoint to this duty." (Acts 6:1–4 ESV)

In the same manner, we must keep our soul healthy by determining who we are called to help. Not every need is ours to meet. If you are able to give, while still having your needs met, then by all means—if you should meet that need—do it. When you are uncertain, pray on it, and if you don't receive anything, weigh it with scripture and move by faith. In this way, you will retain focus and prevent yourself from lacking effectiveness in the needs you must meet, without unnoticeable negligence in meeting your own.

Balance

Being the *yes man* is detrimental to a prospering soul. It often hinges on the neglect of self in a negative way, not to be confused with denying yourself regarding sinful things. Saying *yes* to one thing is also saying *no* to another. For example, if I had the choice to pick between purchasing a white pair of shoes and a blue pair of shoes, saying *yes* to the white pair is saying *no* to the blue pair. In similar manner, saying *yes* to the needs of others when your needs are not met is saying *no* to you. There must be a balance.

With this in mind, it's imperative to discern when we are overcompensating for a missed opportunity, as this too is a form of people-pleasing. If I was unable to meet someone for a business meeting or any kind of mutual form of engagement due to an emergency or something of prevalent importance, it would be appropriate to raincheck and find a later time to meet together. However, it would be inappropriate to schedule multiple rainchecks because I am fueled by regret and fear of losing that relationship, looking at it through the lens of one missed interaction. Given, we must have integrity in our relationships because flaking often becomes an undesirable trait in a healthy and growing relationship.

Practical Examples

Let's say you schedule some much-needed time with your spouse because of a busy work week. It's okay to deny your friends' plea for help as they move into their new house if you have not priorly committed. It is okay to work an extra four hours at the office and not to attend dinner plans with friends because you need to get something done by its deadline. It's okay not to give someone the full amount of money they need because you need to pay for your rent or mortgage. You are not any less of a good friend, employer/employee, or tenant if you say *no* to the *want* in order to say *yes* to the *need*. For this reason, the Word of God says, "For that ye ought to say, If the Lord will, we shall live, and do this, or that" (James 4:15 KJV).

This is where the phrase "God willing" originates. Your needs are a nonnegotiable, and for this purpose, God meets them.

> Therefore do not worry, saying, "What shall we eat?" or "What shall we drink?" or "What shall we wear?" For after all these things the Gentiles seek. For your heavenly Father knows that you need all these things. But seek first the kingdom of God and His righteousness, and

> all these things shall be added to you. Therefore do not worry about tomorrow, for tomorrow will worry about its own things. Sufficient for the day is its own trouble. (Matthew 6:31–34 NKJV)

Put into practice the restraining of self to overpromise. The results are often an underdelivered promise, which can be disappointing to both you and the person you've committed to. Apply James 4:15 in all things, yet do not abuse this safeguard in order to break commitments that you'd like to get out of, which you've previously obligated yourself to. Integrity will make you far more effective in your relationships and does not predicate itself on false hope. Let's reflect the Lord's faithfulness to helping His people by saying what we mean and meaning what we say.

> But let your statement be, 'Yes, yes' or 'No, no'; anything beyond these is of evil. (Matthew 5:37 NASB)

Notice how the word *no* is an option. That means it's okay to choose it when appropriate. Keep in mind, just like there is the *yes man*, the *no man* exists as well. Don't default to either or, but avoid extremes and apply responsibly.

Guilt Trips

Now, one thing to be alert for is the famous guilt trip method. If you are unaware of what a guilt trip is, it's simply when someone makes you feel guilty for not getting their way with you.

This can sometimes be accompanied by hurtful words, threats, gossip, bringing up past favors, etc. Stand firm and do not be moved by subtle and manipulative tactics when others aim to emotionally corner you. This in itself can become a great weight upon your soul and will damage your freedoms, birthing reluctance and resentment.

In conclusion, when you give, do it with a sincere heart and know the following: "A generous person will prosper; whoever refreshes others will be refreshed" (Proverbs 11:25 KJV).

Therefore, do not rob yourself of the provision God has distributed to you to help meet the need of another, when you yourself are not supplied. Do what you can and let God fill in the gaps. Pray for those whom you cannot fully help and ask the Lord to fulfill that need. We are not God; let God be God.

CHAPTER 10

Faith

Why Testing?

If you've ever worked within a corporate setting, marketing, or anything business-related, one of the significant truths you'll learn about obtaining true, long-term success is this: *Success is rarely linear, but instead, divergent.* Let me also assert that this principle is similar in our walks with God, especially when our emotions contend with difficulties, seeking to grasp stability in uncertainty. The ebullience sought after during trials is often found—you guessed it—after trials.

No one likes to suffer, but some seasons are designed to be tough on purpose, although not every difficulty is from God. Contrary to some people's deeply held misconceptions, God is not a cruel tyrant who enjoys watching His children suffer because it pleases Him, in hopes that perhaps faith will arise! That's sadistic and disturbing! In fact, it's often our improper responses to seasons of difficulty, which propel us into needless pain.

When we fail to recognize the season of testing, we fail to maximize its benefits. To put something to the test is to carefully examine its capacities, abilities, and properties in various ways, ensuring that it is able to perform its intended purpose.

When we are tested, it's for us to know what we are made of and for God to show Himself true, in us. Like students who are seated under their teacher's tutelage, studying to prove their knowledge of a particular subject through testing, so our tests reveal not simply what we know, but who we know. Passing the test is dependent on what you've learned and studied from the teacher.

Simplifying the Economic Law of Supply and Demand Spiritually

There is a universal economic law called *the law of supply and demand*. Surplus of supply is often coupled with lower pricing. Increased demand is accompanied by increased pricing. Financial market climates are affected by these general factors. So it is in the spirit.

The welder needs something to weld, the baker must have something to bake, the salesman something to sell, and we need the substance of faith, that we may use it to manifest God's will, in partnership with Him. There is a calling inside of each person, whether it has been discovered or not, which demands the supply of faith to become a reality. Take this excerpt, which exemplifies Abraham's faith in action. Pay attention to the emerging tug of war between supply and demand, glimpsed through the details of the passage:

> Who against hope believed in hope, that he might become the father of many nations, according to that which was spoken, So shall thy seed be. And being not weak in faith, he considered not his own body now dead, when he was about an hundred years old, neither yet the deadness of Sarah's womb: He staggered not at the promise of God through unbelief; but was strong in faith, giving glory to God; And being fully persuaded that, what he had promised, he was able also to perform. And therefore it was imputed to him for righteousness. (Romans 4:18–22 KJV)

The demanding occasion required a supply of faith to rise up and meet it! Faith is essential to our soul because the kingdom of God cannot be received without it! The God-given promises, dreams, and visions which God deeply desires to impregnate us with cannot be birthed by simple logic; they demand faith. This is of extreme importance because our eyes can lead our souls away from the abundance that God has for us. Faith exceeds the bounds of logic, and therefore, we must wrap our minds around faith, instead of wrapping faith around our minds.

What Is Faith and Do You Have It?

> Now faith is the substance of things hoped for, the evidence of things not seen. (Hebrews 11:1 KJV)

This is what Abraham exercised regarding the promises of God, as we've just read! So, where did Abraham get this great faith? Well, these two verses make it clear that it is God Himself who gives us faith!

> Looking unto Jesus the author and finisher of our faith. (Hebrews 11:2 KJV)

> God hath dealt to every man the measure of faith. (Romans 12:3 KJV)

So how is it that others may have more faith than us, since it says that God has given to each person a measure? That's because certain situations demand amassed faith, rather than small amounts.

Think of it in terms of currency. Faith is like a currency that our Heavenly Father made available to us through His Son, Jesus, to pay for things in the spirit, just like we do on earth. In the same way, some things would cost much more than others for various reasons. Since God supplies what we need, the faith which belongs to us will always be there, yet our fears may hinder us from receiving that which has already been graciously given through Jesus. Money, incorrectly stewarded, can subtly diminish in the face of inflation. Now apply this same concept spiritually.

Spiritual inflation can come in the form of business, problems, distractions, unforeseen circumstances, fear, age, family, trauma, and a host of other possibilities. If God has tugged on your heart to perform a task according to His will, it means He's given you the currency of faith to pay for it to manifest.

Faith is the currency Jesus has given us to express what God has impressed, with the help of the Holy Spirit and the church.

When you invest the faith God has given you back into God's vision, you cannot lose. That faith begins to grow, especially if you are actively investing! It is God's divine pleasure to see His children grow and refuse to shrink back in this supernatural currency. Keep investing! We've all been given a choice on how to spend our faith. Remember, some circumstances require more faith than others.

> Now the just shall live by faith: but if any man draw back, my soul shall have no pleasure in him. (Hebrews 10:38 KJV)

How We Think Matters

I recall a moment in prayer a few years prior that granted me a choice in my response to hardship, both present and future. As I was in prayer, this powerful whisper came into my heart from the Lord: "My people want to be more than conquerors, but they want nothing to conquer." When the Lord revealed this to me, I understood that we are so quick to complain, instead of hastening to pray. We are quick to give up, instead of pressing on. We are quick to scurry away from out challenges. We are afraid to lose a battle that has already been won, simply because we cease to walk in the spirit of God and often subjugate ourselves to the lies that the devil produces.

It takes little faith to believe lies, but great faith to conquer them.

> For God has not given us a spirit of fear,
> but of power and of love and of a sound
> mind. (2 Timothy 1:7 KJV)

Therefore, those who are still walking in guilt, shame, condemnation, and powerless works continue *feeling* estranged from God. However, we must walk in the understanding that "there is therefore now no condemnation to them which are in Christ Jesus, who walk not after the flesh, but after the Spirit. For the law of the Spirit of life in Christ Jesus hath made me free from the law of sin and death" (Romans 8:1–2 KJV).

Now knowing these truths, we must recondition our mind to stop circumventing what our heart is so desperately in need of grasping. Our mind should become subservient to the Holy Spirit's leading, as faith is stored up in our heart, not an enemy which pulverizes it through rationalism and logic.

Don't get me wrong. I am not saying "Don't think." In fact, I encourage critical, reflective, observant, and thoughtful thinking as often as possible! If one takes the time to condition their mind to think by faith, we will grow beyond our current capacities in regards to what God deems possible.

For this reason the devil employs disbelief and fear. Fear disables us from walking in the power offered to us by faith, rendering us perpetually ineffective through disbelief. Our enemy is more terrified than we are when we operate by faith, since only then can we partner with God to destroy his kingdom, establishing the kingdom of God. We are not victims; we are the heirs of a victor! Faith is used to obtain the unseen, to overcome the difficult, and to conquer the impossible with Jesus!

The Truth Shall Make You Free

I recently had a friend who confided in me his feeling of condemnation for fifteen years. He questioned his salvation over and over again, continually feeling that he would be eternally separated from God the moment he died. However, I knew that this could not be so, since he would share great revelation that the Holy Ghost would minister to him…and it was in alignment with scripture! Moreover, he confessed and believed "Jesus is Lord" continually.

At this point, I knew he was being oppressed in his thinking. So he fasted and prayed by faith for six days, and on the seventh day, the Holy Spirit granted him powerful revelation that set his mind right. The words he spoke to me were so powerful, I could not keep them to myself. He told me that for fifteen years, he lived under the law, aiming to attain righteousness through his own works. "Since I've lived according to the law, the devil had all the right to accuse me," he stated. I was mind-blown! What a powerful reality the Holy Spirit revealed! Look at what scripture says:

> Howbeit when he, the Spirit of truth, is come, he will guide you into all truth: for he shall not speak of himself; but whatsoever he shall hear, that shall he speak: and he will shew you things to come. (John 16:13 KJV)

> And ye shall know the truth, and the truth shall make you free. (John 8:32 KJV)

We must all stop living life under the law, but instead live under the spirit of life. If we do not, our soul will die daily because we are living as enemies of God when approaching Him in our own righteousness. We cannot repudiate the love of God in Jesus toward us.

> For He made Him who knew no sin to be sin for us, that we might become the righteousness of God in Him. (2 Corinthians 5:21 NKJV)

Jesus was clothed in what the Father hated, in order for us to become what He loved. He was separated from the Father on the cross for a moment, to reconnect us to Him eternally. My friend was just beginning to let this reality sink in.

Nonlinear Faith

Let the chart below represent *A) what we frequently hope and believe our walk with Jesus should be* versus *B) what it actually is.* The linear line represents *A* and the nonlinear line is *B*.

The Word of God is filled with powerful, true stories and examples of the prophets and disciples that went before us, experiencing a nonlinear walk with our Lord. These men and women suffered great tragedies, loss, and even had moments of questioning God's intended purpose for their lives.

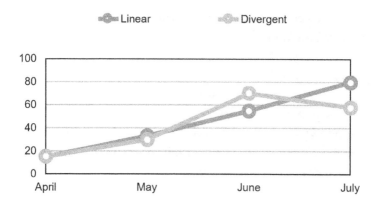

Yet one thing they did not do—give up their faith in Jesus. They pressed beyond what was humanly conceivable to the mind, pushed beyond their fleshly limitations, and by faith, kept walking with God and contending for this great faith we have been given.

Think About What You're Thinking About

Unfortunately, many Christians have suffered from believing the lies of Satan because if he can't cause us to feel condemned, one of his next targets happens to be our confidence.

When we believe the lies of the devil, we forfeit the authority of the truth of God: "For as he thinketh in his heart, so is he" (Proverbs 23:7 KJV).

This is why it is imperative both to guard and renew our mind daily. For this very purpose we need to peer into the magnificent Word of God, the truth that Jesus, along with multitudes of apostles, prophets, pastors, teachers, evangelists, and children of God have literally died to get into our hands. We need to filter lies with truth and believe what God says over how we feel.

Faith must reach into the heart of God, venturing deeply into the realm of fleshly impossibilities, to draw forth the unfathomable realities dreamed of in His heart for us. Whether we are given a glimpse into the future or reminded of great feats the Lord has accomplished in our past, we must draw God's dreams into our present. How?

> But without faith it is impossible to please him: for he that cometh to God must believe that he is, and that he is a rewarder of them that diligently seek him. (Hebrews 11:6 KJV)

Again…faith! If you're like me and have moments where you feel like you have no idea what is going on or perhaps have even lost bits and pieces of faith due to great hardships in life, be encouraged! Since God made this currency, He can supply it. How? Think of this: many children want to purchase a snack or a toy, so they ask their parents. The parent either purchases that thing on their behalf or places the currency in the child's hand to give to the cashier. Most little children don't understand how their parents receive money; they just know that somehow, their needs will be met. They are unaware of their parents' financial hardships, but one thing they know for certain: they can ask, even if the answer is no! They believe that there is a chance for their desire and need to be met!

So what to do when faith is running on E? Simple. We must cry out!

> Immediately the father of the child cried out and said with tears, "Lord, I believe; help my unbelief!" (Mark 9:24 NKJV)

We must ask our Father for help in prayer, humbly. God desires us to have faith more than we do! When we start believing His voice, word, commandments, and instructions, made effective by our actions, our mind-sets become molded by a living faith. When we look to Jesus, we can start thinking from heaven down. Mind-set is the trajectory of our faith. If we believe we can't, we often won't. However, if we believe God can do the impossible through us, then we will truly be more than conquerors, just like the miraculous stories we read in His Word. The impossible is accomplished by faith in Jesus, the Son of God!

> Now unto him that is able to do exceeding abundantly above all that we ask or think, according to the power that worketh in us, Unto him be glory in the church by Christ Jesus throughout all ages, world without end. Amen. (Ephesians 3:20–21 KJV)

Our souls are deeply affected by what we think, what we believe, and what we do. Think faith, believe by faith, do by faith. We all need it.

CHAPTER 11

Change Your Angle

I can't describe to you the excitement of what I'm about to share, but it feels like a grown man has butterflies in his stomach. These stories are authentic, real, and beneficial for you to learn from. They are my own experiences and have shaped the way I view some things of God. Enjoy!

Successful for a Season

When I was in my early twenties, I was constantly finding myself in a state of what I perceived was failure. The perennial issue I was having involved starting something with a group of people for Jesus...and then that group eventually diminishing for whatever reason. These instances would leave me distraught all too often.

One day a friend and I were meeting at a bagel shop in Santa Clarita, California. During our time together, I confided in her that I felt like a failure, especially when it came to the things of God. I explained how as a teenager, I had a Christian dance crew that eventually fell apart and that as a gospel rap artist, I was a part of a group that also ended up splitting.

As I expressed these things, the label of failure kept swarming around me, looking for a place to land in my soul…and it started creating a hive of insecurity within my heart. It stung me every time I thought I failed at something. Specific memories would torment me with the label of failure's offspring—screw up. I did not know how to wage war against these thoughts.

But this encounter with my friend was a game changer, a one-line sucker punch of great wisdom and revelation to my soul that Jesus Himself must have orchestrated because that one-liner has not left me since. She simply stated the following, as best as I can remember: "God has not called you to be tied down to one group, but desires to use you to work with many different kinds of people, churches, and organizations. You did not fail, you were successful for a season."

I was in utter disbelief! Could what she said actually be true? It resonated so deeply within my person that it changed the way I view the things of God. What Satan kept using to disqualify me was an actual graduation present from my Heavenly Father! I had absolutely no idea! His Word even says, "He has made everything beautiful in its time"(Ecclesiastes 3:11 NKJV).

Why was I in the dark for so long? Some of you may be reading this and may be welling up with tears of joy, relief, or resting in the fact that someone understands. I promise you Jesus does and He is not absent-minded of how you feel when you thought things didn't work out.

Failing Is Not Failure

Failure is part of the road to success, provided that we learn from our mistakes and apply the corrections made in our affliction. Failing in one area doesn't make you a failure in all areas, the same way that succeeding at one thing doesn't make you successful at all things. Failing does not produce failure; however, our response to failing can. It is imperative to be resilient through the most difficult of times and to persist with a proper response to what we perceive as *failure*.

The right response can determine the right results. A lack of veracity regarding how we view ourselves in light of failure can significantly skew how we truly see ourselves and others who fail. If we believe we are failures, then failure is what we will produce. Therefore, we must guard our heart and mind from seeping emotional instability, combating it with the truth of God.

Change Your Angle

I remember back in 2010, I felt God calling me out of the church I was currently attending. I was living in Santa Clarita, California, at the time and was attending a church in Van Nuys, California, called The Church on the Way. In fact, this is the church where I surrendered my life to Jesus as a youth. I was also dating a young lady at the time who invited me to her church in Newhall, California, and so I began attending there as well. On yet another occasion, some friends invited me to check out a church, also in Newhall, California, at the time named New Life in His Presence.

At the time I went to visit, it was about one year old, and my first conversation with the senior pastor was something along the lines of "Where are you going to church?" I explained that I was between multiple churches and was already feeling called away from the first one. He hit me with a scripture: "'Those who are planted in the house of the Lord shall flourish' (Psalm 92:13 NKJV). You need to plant somewhere in order to grow. You can't be between multiple churches. I am not telling you to come here, but pray and see where you should plant."

I knew His instruction was sound and quickly applied what I had just learned through our conversation. On my drive home, I parked my car in a special spot that the Lord and I would often speak. I presented my dilemma of the three churches to Him and asked Him where to go. He told me to start attending New Life in His Presence, which is now called Elevate Church. Now you may not believe what I am about to tell you, but with all my heart, I promise this is the truth. I heard the Lord tell me, "I am going to prove it to you. Go lay down on your driveway and look at the stars for ten minutes. I am going to send you a shooting star within that time frame, and this will be your sign to attend New Life." This was not uncommon because I would often do this, but never with a time frame or a promise attached to it. As it grew late in the evening, I sat still in my car to ponder what I had just heard. Then the Lord reiterated a word that the pastor had spoken that previous Sunday: "Delayed obedience is disobedience. I said go!"

There was a sense of urgency in the way the Lord spoke, so I departed from the location quickly, drove home, parked my car, laid out on the driveway, and put my phone timer on for a ten-minute countdown. At five minutes, I noticed clouds rolling in and began to doubt if I had actually heard from Almighty God or if my mind was manufacturing a voice and labeling it God. As soon as I observed the clouds, anxiety began to creep up on me. I heard in my heart the words "Change your angle."

These words ricocheted off of the walls of my being and would not stop until I was compelled to literally look in the opposite direction. What do you know…it was clear skies where the stars were actually visible. Six minutes went by, then seven minutes, and up till this point…no shooting star. By minute eight I began to worry. I cried out to God, "Lord, if you want me to go to this church, then show me your mighty power and let me see the shooting star."

Then suddenly between the end of minute eight and the beginning of minute nine, I saw the shooting star God promised. I began to weep and knew that God had indeed spoken to me and qualified His voice with the simplest of wonders. I was utterly shocked and amazed that I was valued that much! God desired to lead me to where He destined for me to plant myself.

I spent eight and a half years at that church and served for at least seven of them in some form of leadership. It was one of the best decisions I was ever led to make in my entire existence. Therefore, in the same way that I was instructed to change my angle, it's important to determine the truth about your life by the correct perceptions. Are you really a failure or just successful for a season?

You see…it's not about what people think of you. Today someone may champion you, only to change their perceptions of you tomorrow. They may speak well of you, only to assassinate your character at a later date. The truth is, we can never please people, so why start the arduous journey of aiming to fit their mold? What matters the most is what God thinks of you and what you think of yourself. Last time I checked, failure was not in God's vocabulary as a definition for His creation. So then, why is it in yours?

CHAPTER 12

We Need Jesus

As our time together comes to a close, your time with Jesus does not have to. The prospering soul is contingent on relationship with Him, application of His instruction, and continuing many of the methods presented in the first part of this book. Although it would take many books to even scratch the surface of the fullness of how to fully make the soul prosper, encapsulating a host of other tactics, may these writings serve you well as a start. In no way do I claim to have full knowledge and understanding of any matter in life; however, I hope that my experiences shared with you in this book helped to shed a brighter light in some dimly lit areas.

Now for those who have diligently read this book and have longed for a relationship with Jesus, knowing about Him yet never really knowing Him, please lend me your eyes and ears for this last chapter. If you receive nothing else from this book, *this is the most important thing you can take away.* We've saved the best for last! Whether you believe this or not, agree or not, hate this or not, I plead with you to take these words seriously. They will serve as a witness for you or against you.

You may be wondering what I'm talking about, as in previous chapters, but I will be unapologetically blunt. Many reading this book have grown up in Christian homes or church, while others have not. You may have stumbled upon this book and desired to read something purposeful, without giving it much thought. Some may have abandoned the faith and picked this up simply to criticize and aim to shoot down what seems irrational or illogical. However, this invitation belongs to those who will accept it and cannot be forced, guilt-tripped, or anything other than lovingly offered to you.

It does not require a scholar to know that this life is short and that eternity is exactly what it sounds like—eternal. The truth is, every one of us has done something wrong, whether that's lying, stealing, cheating, pre-marital sex (of any sort), cursing, gossip, etc. Why do I bring this up? These habits and behaviors are ungodly and are called sin; sin being the chosen expression of evil, revealed to us by the laws God gave Moses to govern Israel with. These laws were to expose sin, to set the standard of God's righteousness, and to exalt the truth above all opinion. All of us have partaken in sin and have hurt ourselves and maybe even those around us in doing so.

Usually, this takes place when we disregard what God thinks and how He feels about the situation, casting His laws behind us. This literally causes us to oppose the one who loves us more than anyone or anything we've ever experienced, neglecting His instruction. We know His laws and commandments through the Holy Bible. This was written through men, by God, so that men would be without excuse on the day we stand before Him who will judge us for the lives we've lived upon the earth.

So what about those who've never read the Word of God? Well, that is why God placed a moral compass hidden in the conscience of man. He's the one who has presented our hearts with the reality of eternity and the curiosity which surrounds it. He's the inventor of the *gut feeling*! He's the one who grieves often, but not always, silently hoping, waiting, and longing for us to draw close and deciphering the trail of breadcrumbs that lead to Him. These breadcrumbs include the majesty displayed in nature, the random act of kindness toward you, the avoiding of the car accident, the saving of your life in the accident, the personal breakthroughs your heart has cried out for that your lips never confessed—all of these signs are pointing to someone. His name is Jesus or Yeshua (Hebrew).

He created a system for life, contained in the blood of all living things; even trees or leaves contain sap and run through a series of veins that nourishes the organism. However, the Holy Bible says:

> For all have sinned and come short of the glory of God. (Romans 3:23 KJV)

> For the wages of sin is death; but the gift of God is eternal life through Jesus Christ our Lord. (Romans 6:23 KJV)

You see, over 2,000 years ago, a sacrifice was made on your behalf. Our Heavenly Father knew that we could never repay the accumulating debt that we owed Him, due to our sins. Therefore, Jesus, His only Son, being fully God, came to the earth to experience life as a man, living it to the perfect standard of God, where everyone else fell short. He gave Himself into the hands of those He made, being crucified upon a cross for you and I, as those who crucified Him were blinded from recognizing their salvation. He did this out of His own free will because the only way to pacify the death that clung to you and I was to give it something else to kill, until it was conquered. You may be thinking, "Why did God create death?"

The truth is He didn't; mankind did. In the entirety of the creation story (Genesis 1 and 2), death was mentioned once (v. 17) as a warning for man to avoid. God literally told man that His sin would create the entity and phenomenon of death, but mankind was tempted by the devil to disobey God, falling into sin, causing it to affect all things under mankind's dominion (including man made in God's image). Satan, who was cast down to the earth for trespassing against God in heaven (Revelation 12), is the father of death.

Genesis 3 reveals how he, knowing the plight that would befall mankind, would cause them to lose their first estate as he did. In fact, God knew that as soon as the accuser of His children would be cast out of heaven and into the earth, that Jesus was going to embark on the greatest of all rescue missions. Jesus Himself knew this to be true (Luke 10:17–20).

As prophets, priests, and holy men who lived hundreds of years before Jesus made declarations by the Holy Spirit about who mankind's savior would be, where He would be born, and the purpose for His arrival, sin ran rampant. In the waiting, people began to and still do worship things created by mankind, becoming blinded to the reality of God, due to the constant indulging of sin. So how can we be sure that God really did send His Son to save us?

History, archeology, astronomy, medical research, eyewitness testimonies, revelation, and the supernatural all attest to this truth as well. You are not being hoaxed! Whoever lied to you or told you that heaven and hell are figments of your imaginations are one of three things: 1) a liar; 2) ignorant of the truth; or 3) don't think you're worth saving! Whoever has persuaded you with their bias, explaining away the deity of Jesus, masking it with claims that He was simply an extraordinary revolutionary, has missed the gospel entirely! In addition, if someone has told you that you can sin habitually and disregard holiness because of grace, they have fed you lies that, if believed, will place you in grave danger!

Jesus is the only way for our sins to be forgiven. His blood was the only uncorrupted bloodline that could pacify the sins of all of mankind. Why? Please read *Romans 5*; my explanation is simply far too subpar in comparison with God's. Paraphrased: One man sinned and brought death upon all…one man lived perfectly, giving His life to conquer it for all. The reason being that sin produces death. The sinless cannot die (since there is no death produced); therefore, He continually lives (being full of life), not only as a man, but resurrected bodily unto God, giving of His life by the Holy Spirit, to those who put their faith in Him.

This may not make much sense yet, but we're almost there. Since sin is conceived in the heart of man, that is the exact location where the salvation of God makes its introduction. For this purpose, it is stated: "That if you confess with your mouth the Lord Jesus and believe in your heart that God has raised Him from the dead, you will be saved. For with the heart one believes unto righteousness, and with the mouth confession is made unto salvation" (Romans 10:9 NKJV).

A confession is powerless unless accompanied by an action.

The action God requires of people is to leave willful and purposeful sin behind, striving to live according to His will, empowered by the Holy Spirit. The temptation and lie of the devil is to believe that we firstly need to get clean before we come to God, that somehow we have the power to lay hold of our own righteousness. The truth is we simply can't obtain righteousness in our own ability. We need Jesus!

> Nevertheless the foundation of God standeth sure, having this seal, The Lord knoweth them that are his. And, Let everyone that nameth the name of Christ depart from iniquity. (2 Timothy 2:19 KJV)

Now, please note that God is not excluding other faiths, people groups, or individuals from salvation. In fact, He's inviting everyone to partake, through His Son. The rejection of the Christ is the entrance to eternal damnation. As God warned in the garden, so through these words, God, because of His great love for you, is warning you. Hell is not God's heart for you or anyone around you; it was literally created for the devil and his angels (Matthew 25:41).

This is not a fear tactic, nor is it a guilt trip! It's the epitome of love's appeal for the salvation of your soul. Whether you've never asked Jesus to save you or whether you have and walked away, you absolutely cannot prosper, knowing that you are already condemned (John 3:16–21). I beg you, please…receive the precious life that Jesus so dearly paid for. He literally died for you to have the best life possible (John 10:10). If you are feeling anxious, with your heart quickly beating, feeling drawn by these words, please know that God is calling you. You don't need to know everything all at once. You simply need to know that someone wants to do life with you, save you from hell, and empower you to help others do the same. If you're not feeling anything, but desire this, God is also calling you. He calls us to know Him, not feel Him. Therefore, If you are willing to take Jesus up on this offer, please pray this out loud and believe with your heart, or pray with your own words unto God.

> Lord Jesus, I believe that You are the Son of God and that You alone can save me from my sin. I believe that God has raised You from the dead, in the flesh, and according to Your Word, You will save my soul from sin, death, and hell if I depart from it.
>
> However, Lord, only You have the power to liberate me from this bondage. Please save me, set me free, and fill me with your Holy Spirit. Thank You for the forgiveness of my sins, I receive it. I believe that I have been made right before the Father and that His wrath against my

sin is pacified. Jesus, thank You for separating me from darkness and calling me into the light. I'm Yours now.

If you've prayed this prayer, you are now a new creation. Your old life has passed, and new life has come into you. Your next steps include reading the Holy Bible, getting plugged into a local church, and continued prayer. If you're up to it, you may get baptized. Make sure to find healthy Christlike mentors and surround yourself with strong brothers and sisters in the faith. As these steps are taken, know that you've been invited into the best relationship you'll ever be in and into the greatest journey you'll undertake.

Now, you are able to join the rescue mission to see souls prosper all over the world in Jesus, for Jesus. God bless you as your soul continues to thrive in Him.

> Let us hear the conclusion of the whole matter: Fear God, and keep his commandments: for this is the whole duty of man. For God shall bring every work into judgment, with every secret thing, whether it be good, or whether it be evil. (Ecclesiastes 12:13–14 KJV)

> Beloved, I wish above all things that thou mayest prosper and be in health, even as thy soul prospereth. (3 John 1:2 KJV)

ABOUT THE AUTHOR

Born and raised in Toronto, Canada, Benjamin Gideon moved to Los Angeles, California, with his family at the age of eleven. After having a powerful encounter with Jesus at the age of thirteen, he dedicated his life to serving God. Since then, he has had many powerful encounters that continue to fuel his deeply held convictions and love for Christ. He is currently the lead pastor of Rest in Grace Church in Santa Clarita, California, and is co-president of his family's fastener business, Advance Fasteners Inc.

Along with the aforementioned, Benjamin's background in the entertainment industry as a gospel rapper and a film student have been some of the platforms he's used to creatively preach the gospel, allowing for events with the American Cancer Society, the National Association for the Advancement of Colored People (NAACP), and the Los Angeles County Sheriff's Department. Benjamin graduated from California State University of Northridge in 2016, with a Bachelor's Degree in Cinema and Television Arts. The deepest cry of his heart is to see the church become a worthy bride for her husband and king—the Lord Jesus.

CPSIA information can be obtained
at www.ICGtesting.com
Printed in the USA
BVHW041146110723
667064BV00002B/239